Secondary Education

Kathy Vandyck has been teaching English since 1991. After graduating from Emmanuel College, Cambridge, she first worked as a press and information officer in the Department of Education and Science and the Home Office. She completed her PGCE at King's College, London, and has taught in London comprehensives since qualifying. She was assistant head of department, but is currently working part-time, having had a baby in 1997.

Secondary Education

Kathy Vandyck

FOURTH ESTATE • *London*

First published in Great Britain in 1999 by
Fourth Estate Limited
6 Salem Road
London W2 4BU

Copyright © 1999 Fourth Estate Limited

10 9 8 7 6 5 4 3 2 1

The right of Kathy Vandyck to be identified as the author of this work has been asserted by her in accordance with the Copyright, Designs and Patents Act 1988

ISBN 1-85702-750-7

All rights reserved. No part of this publication may be reproduced, transmitted, or stored in a retrieval system, in any form or by any means, without permission in writing from Fourth Estate Limited.

Typeset by York House Typographic Ltd, London
Printed in Great Britain by Clays Ltd, St Ives plc, Bungay, Suffolk

Contents

Introduction   **1**

1 Classroom Teaching   **3**

Working with children – Working with your subject – Working with adults – Pound signs and professional pride – Staff development and training – How to stay fresh

2 Breaking In   **25**

Getting a taster – Getting qualified – Courses – Making your training applications – Course interviews – The course – Getting a job – First job, first school – Interviews

3 Choosing Your School   **50**

How to find out whether a school is 'good' – Types of school – LEA schools – Comprehensives – Grant-maintained schools – Independent schools – Voluntary schools – Single-sex schools – Specific age-range schools – Selective schools – Community schools – Special schools – Specialist schools

4 Chalk Another One Up: Career Progression   **77**

Promotion – Points – Prospects – Positions – Senior management – Middle management – Other posts of responsibility

Secondary Education

5 Homework, and Leaving School   99

Part-time and job-shares – Secondments and career breaks – Different phases – Different pupils – Supply teaching – Tutoring – Specialist support teaching – Examining – Training and advisory work – Inspection – Textbook writing – Other careers

6 Blackboards Abroad   125

Teacher exchange – Non-exchange teaching posts – Voluntary teaching – Teaching English abroad

Appendix A: **Useful Addresses**   135

Appendix B: **Points Systems and Pay Scales**   145

Acknowledgements   150

Introduction

Why teach in a secondary school? Here's the quick answer, for the short term. The job is stimulating and multi-faceted, with more than its fair share of day-to-day interest. You spend your working life with lively young people and committed, able colleagues. You get the rare job satisfaction (and pressure) of doing a job which is worthwhile and matters, to individual children and society. The workload intrudes too often into your own life. The pay could be better. But the holidays are a bonus.

If that sounds like an acceptable balance of pros and cons, then teaching may be the profession for you in the long term too. The picture is again not perfect, but it does have significant attractions. For many, teaching holds enough challenge to repay a lifetime spent purely in the classroom, although the financial rewards and career structures of the classroom practitioner need attention. For those who want to manage schools as well as classrooms, prospects are clearer and better paid. Management jobs are challenging and important, with anti-social working hours to match. As the shape of the working day and year provides some inherent flexibility, it is also a career which can cope with changes in your personal circumstances – not to mention geography. (In an age of more diverse working patterns, more could be done, however, to accommodate teachers who want to study, broaden their experience, or make temporary changes to their work practices. It is in everyone's interests to keep teachers learning and working.) Lastly, if recent retirement patterns are a good guide, full-time classroom teaching may not be the ideal job for your later years. But as new pension arrangements mean older teachers won't now have the option of retiring early, there may be some interesting developments in how teachers work at the end of their careers. Opportunities for teaching-related employment are certainly there, if limited in number at present, and teaching does fit you out with lots of useful and transferable skills.

With education high on the national and international agenda, it's an interesting time for the profession, too. The demand for teachers may – who knows? – lead to some of the drawbacks of the job being dealt with. Projections are that 50 per cent more secondary teachers will be needed by 2000, and demand in shortage subjects like maths, science, information and design technology, and modern languages will be especially keen. The Teacher Training Agency (TTA), established to feed teacher demand, is putting much of its efforts into promoting a positive image of the profession. In addition, there are funded measures like taster courses and access courses, also designed to attract badly needed teachers from under-represented groups like the ethnic communities. A more coherent structure for professional development is on its way, with qualifications and training as staging posts along the route of a teacher's career, not just at the beginning. There will be a General Teaching Council, trailed for years as the only way to raise the status of teaching to match that of other professions, like medicine. Finally, the Green Paper claims it will reward good teachers through a new career structure linked to pay. It promises better working environments and support for teachers.

The concrete results of all this potential improvement remain to be seen. Pay is still a stumbling block for many who would otherwise be drawn to teaching; whether the under-representation of men in non-managerial classroom teaching is the cause or the result of low pay is an interesting question. But there's nothing more depressing than a staffroom cynic, and the next few years may hold some pleasant surprises for an already attractive career. Look at it this way – if over 200,000 people already do the job despite sometimes appalling PR, lack of expense accounts and prehistoric workplaces, ask yourself why . . .

Classroom Teaching

'OK, so I've got through the first term. But now I've actually got to teach them something!'
Newly qualified drama teacher, staggering tired and emotional into the Christmas holidays

The thing about teaching is that there is rather a lot going on at once, so you need above all to be flexible. You fulfil a number of roles, as in secondary school you are three types of teacher at once – subject specialist, form tutor and more generally a member of staff, who communicates the school's messages about learning and the adult world. Depending on what sort of teacher you are speaking to, and the sort of school they teach in, the order of importance of these three roles will probably vary. A grammar-school teacher might see herself primarily as a subject expert, whilst a teacher in a deprived area might see his pastoral role or general role as educator as being more prominent; part of the interest of a career in teaching comes from shifting the emphasis as you move from lesson to lesson, post to post and school to school. But wherever you see your priorities lying, all three come into play. Next, there are a host of different skills involved. Performing, managing, administrating, counselling – you can find yourself having to draw on all these in the classroom. If you don't like having to keep lots of balls in the air at once, you probably wouldn't enjoy a day in a school.

And finally, you need to be self-policing. Teaching is a high-profile job and it matters if you are doing it badly; people notice, and rightly so. But what's perhaps less obvious to onlookers (and more relevant to a work-force who are overwhelmingly conscientious) is that teachers expect to be fine-tuning their work constantly, even when it's going well. Although it's a very public profession, there is a great deal of autonomy in the classroom, so you have to be able and willing to reflect on your own working practices and make your own improvements. The majority of the time, teachers need to provide their own inspiration and be their own critics. As the drama teacher's quote shows, you can feel that no sooner have you got one aspect of the job sorted, than another presents itself; moments of smugness tend to be brief.

If this sounds a bit daunting, it is; that's the interest of the job. It is the diversity and constant challenge of teaching which provides its attractions as a long-term career. And thankfully, there are actual duties to be done to take your mind off what you're not doing. These are set out in the Schoolteachers' Pay and Conditions Document, and range from the obvious (teaching, planning lessons, marking) to the less well-known tasks of providing careers advice, covering absent colleagues and ordering equipment. You can meet 150 individuals in a day, face any number of situations the moment you walk through the staffroom or classroom door, and feel like all your skills and faculties have been stretched. You have the satisfaction of knowing that what you do is useful and worthwhile. And if you can find a way of lightening a proper sense of responsibility with a little self-preservation, it can also be a real laugh.

The Pay and Conditions Document also gives an insight into the sort of working life teachers lead. Full-time teachers must 'be available for work for 195 days in any year, of which 190 days shall be days on which they may be required to teach pupils in addition to carrying out other duties; and those 195 days shall be specified by the employer, or if the employer directs, by the headteacher'. As these stipulations suggest, teachers work to timetables, bells and calendars. There is considerable autonomy and unpredictability in some areas of the job, but when you turn up is not down to you. If you're a teacher you must expect always to go on holiday in August, and expect always, for at least a year, to see the same faces on a Tuesday morning at 10.06 a.m.

On those 195 days, teachers must 'perform such duties at such times and such places as may be specified by the headteacher for 1265 hours in any one year, these hours to be allocated reasonably throughout those days in the year on which teachers are required to be available for work'. These 1265 hours are 'directed time' when, as the name suggests, teachers carry out work according to the head's directions. The School Teachers' Review Body, which published its latest report in February 1997, gives a breakdown of how much time is spent on what, based on a snapshot in March 1996. The majority of class teachers' time – 41.5 per cent – is spent on teaching lessons; almost another 30 per cent is spent preparing and marking. A further 11 per cent is spent dealing with pupils and parents outside lessons, and 6 per cent dealing with colleagues. The final 11.5 per cent goes on administration – the dreaded 'paperwork' – and individual activity.

Given this breakdown, it helps if you are good at managing your own time, as so much of your work – 70 per cent – is autonomous, albeit within a very fixed structure; it's a curious mix of working conditions. In a 'reasonable' school, there will be some discussion as to how and where the collective hours are spent. For example, the staff might be consulted on how to spread parents' evenings, or administrative meetings which take place after school. After that, you must be able to organise yourself accordingly, and be willing to respond to the calendar rather than follow your own priorities. Good organisation is extremely important in the classroom, and out of it. You can't set a crucial GCSE assessment test a week after 11B's reports are due to be written; forward planning not only makes life easier for you, but in a complex network like a school, you have to be sensitive to the difficulties you cause your colleagues if you don't meet deadlines. One editor for an educational publisher says: 'You can always tell whether a textbook has been written by an academic or a schoolteacher; teachers always get their manuscripts in on time.'

The good news is that the headteacher doesn't necessarily fill all 1265 hours with specified tasks. The reason for this is that teachers work way beyond this statutory number, and a recent Review Body survey recorded a working week closer to double the statutory hours. In secondary schools, classroom teachers worked on average fifty hours a week, heads of department worked fifty-three hours, deputies put in fifty-six hours and heads sixty-two hours. More than 25 per cent of these hours are worked outside the 'school day' (after 6 p.m. or at weekends). This is not surprising when you realise that directed time doesn't cover essential tasks like marking and preparation, let alone parents' evenings, the voluntary meetings – say on curriculum development – or extra-curricular activities which make for a professionally run and active school. Teaching is hard work both mentally and physically, and this is why the line 'But you finish at 3.30 p.m. ... ' is guaranteed to annoy even the mildest of the profession's members.

Having said that, it is in fact true that you can go home at 3.30 p.m., at least at the moment. Watch this space for rumblings about major restructuring of the school year, to bring teachers' days and holidays much closer to the office 'norm'. In these days when working culture often demands that you be seen at your desk well into the evening (whether you're being productive or not), it's nice to be in control of your own time. A head of geography makes the point: 'I know it's not fashionable to say so, but as a career for a working mother, teaching takes some beating. On a day when there are no meetings, I can be home with my daughter at 4 p.m. and spend the rest of the day with her. The hard part is that at 8 p.m. when she goes to bed, I have to start working. But I get to choose.' And this freedom isn't handy only for traditional domestic reasons; one entrepreneurial teacher with a passion for stand-up manages to run a once-a-week comedy club in the hours when he isn't teaching. The same is true of holidays. Although the notion that 'what you do with the other half of the year' is up for grabs is sadly mistaken, as teachers routinely use their holidays to catch up on what they couldn't fit into busy school terms, having unusually long blocks of time away from the workplace is a rare luxury. With forward planning, you can spend five weeks in the summer trekking in Borneo, teaching soccer in Camp America, or playing with your kids. As one young teacher says: 'I used to get very hot under the collar when people started on about "all those holidays".

Now, I just say "Yeah, it's great, isn't it?" and make sure I've arranged something that will make them really jealous. They're right – it's a great perk.'

WORKING WITH CHILDREN

Teaching is about dealing with people. Obviously it's not a job for the sociopath or prohibitively shy, and it must be said that most teachers (and all happy ones) actively like the company of the children they teach. And of course with secondary teaching, for 'children' read a whole range of people, from shiny, happy eleven year olds, to fifteen year olds forging their own identities, to fully formed young adults in your A level classes. It is this range of age groups and numbers of pupils which attracts many to secondary teaching, where, every academic year, you can be responsible for the progress of up to thirty children in each year group. (Primary teaching offers a more intense, all-round involvement with far fewer individuals every working year, and more specialisation in the education of specific year groups across a teacher's career.) In a secondary, you spend your working days with people who are at exciting and difficult times in their lives, and all ages present their own rewards and challenges, and require different handling. In terms of skills, you need to be both confident and sensitive to others, because you are dealing with two constituencies in a classroom: the group and the individual.

The mention of most jobs triggers a standard response. If you're a lawyer, you'll probably be told about a fence dispute, or asked how you can defend a guilty person; if you're a writer, you'll be regaled with lots of 'hilarious' anecdotes, on the basis 'you could write a play about this'. Say you're a teacher, and a comment about holidays will probably follow, but say you're a secondary teacher, and you hear: 'Ooh, you're brave! I don't think I could handle a class of fifteen year olds.' Managing a class is often perceived by outsiders as the most challenging task of the teacher and although this is a superficial view, you do need to want to be in control. The group, like most groups, is more Neanderthal in its behaviour and needs more basic messages than the individual. An experienced head of department whose hard-man image precedes him like a bouncer into every classroom, and who began his teaching career in a particularly troubled inner-city school says: 'I used to box when I was young and it taught me some useful lessons in handling kids – get them before they get you.'

This may not be everyone's approach (and it is important to know that the same teacher is popular because of his equally strong reputation for fairness), but a healthy respect for group dynamics is needed. Looked at more positively, there can be real satisfaction in creating unity and purpose within a large group, and harnessing a class's goodwill and co-operation. One experienced teacher who spends less and less time in the classroom says: 'I miss the buzz of leading a class, of striking up a rapport with and within a group.' And every class – and most year groups – has its own personality, which is fun to get to know and know how to work with. This is why teaching exactly the same syllabus over a number of years, or to more than one group in the same year group, can still be interesting.

Discipline relies on many factors, not a mystic ability to freeze a teenager at fifty paces. Knowing your class, good organisation and pace, a well-thought-out lesson which meets the children's needs – these are, in the long term, all more important and effective means of control than a loud voice. And crowd control is only a means to an end: 'I'm strict only so that I can get the kind of classroom I want – a pleasant working environment,' says a formidable Head of RE. Few teachers get deep satisfaction from their more macho encounters with young people; it's the individuals who make up the crowd who count and who are most frequently mentioned when teachers talk about job satisfaction. A typical sentiment comes from a teacher speaking of a fifth year in her support group: 'Right now, I'm on tenterhooks waiting for the re-sit results. Every day I approach my pigeonhole with trepidation ... he missed by three marks last time, and if he gets through it'll be the highlight of my year.' In terms of your interpersonal skills, it's also the individual who requires the more subtle and interesting psychological handling. The rewards are substantial when you finally figure out a way of motivating a child who's convinced herself she 'can't do science' and of rewarding the fifteen year old who wants to do well, is doing well, but can't let his mates see that he is.

Knowing how to deal with people comes to a large extent from experience, and having a tried and tested bag of tricks, but teaching is a career where you can use your personality. Many teachers value the fact that they are not only drawing on professional skills, but on their individuality and experiences: 'I basically teach in the way my mother brought us up; she's my greatest influence, not what I learnt at training college,' says one. A sense of humour is always mentioned by pupils as being important, but thankfully you don't have to conform to a blueprint; all sorts of personalities make good teachers. 'Individual pupils respond better to individual teachers – it's perfectly natural. So it's only right that there should be a broad spectrum of personalities in teaching, to give young people a choice of what sort of adult they want to be,' said a head of year. Extra-curricular activities often play a large part in showing them a more human side.

It's not a job where you can 'just be yourself', however. In the same way as there's a lot of autonomy but lots of fixed structure in the work, you have to balance accessibility and professional distance. Whether you like it or not, you're a role model and represent the values of the school. Teenagers are acutely aware of hypocrisy so if you're bending the rules on timekeeping, it will be difficult for you to lay down the law, and it's important to be aware of your own foibles and prejudices. You are never off duty, and some teachers find this a pressure, especially if they believe their public role extends not just into the corridor and car park but, according to some commentators, far into the community beyond, like some kind of moral fire-fighters.

WORKING WITH YOUR SUBJECT

When asked, pupils generally say they want a teacher who is in control and friendly; the third quality they mention is 'being able to explain'. Education minister Robin Squire announced in 1996, 'From structural changes, educational debate is now shifting to pedagogy – how to make sure improvements are secured through effective teaching in every classroom' and government focus is still firmly on standards of teaching and learning. For all those teachers desperate to get back to the real business of schools, this was very welcome: 'The bottom line is that you want to see your kids do well,' says one head of department.

Teaching in both secondary and primary phases comes down to an enjoyment of seeing children learn, achieve and develop. What's distinctive about teaching at the secondary level is subject specialism, and the opportunity to share an expertise and enthusiasm for a particular subject is what draws many teachers to this age group. Primary teachers are tremendously impressive in the way that they inspire their pupils and foster their competence in a range of subject areas, but if your real love lies in one particular subject, secondary teaching is for you. And not only does teaching test what you really know about your subject, but it allows you to develop your interests and you can find fresh ways of looking at topics through your pupils, especially in upper school and sixth-form teaching. In secondary teaching, you're also privy to teenagers' ideas, opinions and emotions, and the strength of these can add zest to your subject material.

The National Curriculum lays down criteria for what children should be able to 'know, understand and be able to do', and the same trinity is on the agenda for teachers. First, you must understand your subject. Next, you have to know where you are taking your class and the individuals in it over a course of lessons and terms: there has to be precision in your aims, so you know exactly what you are trying to convey or get them to explore, at the right level for the children in the class. Finally, you must be able to execute these plans – the learning must actually take place in the lesson – and respond with a bit of flexibility, to cope with unforeseen circumstances. The National Curriculum sets out the skills and subject areas which pupils must cover, but there is still considerable freedom for teachers in how they teach the material. How to match the tasks to the class, present a dry topic or build a course round an exam syllabus is a matter for teachers and departments.

Whether you are successful can be judged from the interest and success of your pupils, their qualifications, but also their own improvement and progress, so a willingness to question your methods is essential – you need to be prepared to experiment and reflect. One of the most impressive qualities of good teachers is that they are never complacent and the TTA's criteria for new teachers includes 'The need to take responsibility for [one's] own professional development'. The range of skills involved in classroom teaching is broad – academic, practical, analytical, intuitive, organisational – and few mortals can achieve a perfect synthesis. It's realistic to expect strengths and weaknesses in your overall performance, and important to strike a balance. Be prepared, but also be ready for a change of plan. Find what suits you, but be aware there are other ways of doing things.

The subject you teach can also make your experience of teaching quite different to a colleague in the same school and affect the most basic aspects of your work life – your timetable, the pattern of your hours and workload, your pay – as well as the more qualitative aspects like your relationship with pupils, the attitudes of parents and the atmosphere of your department. For example, Helen, a maths specialist of two years' experience, teaches a timetable consisting of a single class in every year, from Year 7 to A level. She sees each class about three times a week and knows a lot about each of her pupils, which will stand her in good stead for open evenings, when most of her pupils' parents will want to find her for an in-depth chat. In her GCSE class, she teaches a couple of characters who '' 'ate maths and didn't wanna do it' but most of them know they need a decent grade to get them onto their chosen courses of training schemes and attend the revision class she runs at lunch-time. She works in a department of seven, and although her immediate boss is the Head of Maths, she works closely with the Key Stage 3 Co-ordinator on lower-school issues, like the compulsory National Curriculum tests coming up for all her Year 9 pupils; there's a lot of pressure on the department to raise results from last year. She is about to take charge of plans for using IT in maths, and this will bring her first responsibility point.

Contrast this with Jim, who works in the Religious Studies department. It's a small, two-person department and his head of department is on one more responsibility point than Helen after ten years in teaching. He used to have to decide which meetings to attend, as he was in theory working to three different managers when he also taught history and sociology. This year, however, his timetable is solid RS, and he has four classes in some lower-school years; this saves on preparation as he teaches the same course to each class, but reporting can be stressful as he has to write about 120 pupils at the same time. He enjoys seeing how the same topic goes down with different classes, and feels that his contact with whole year groups will help him pursue a pastoral deputy job. He doesn't teach A level as it isn't offered in RS in his school. He sometimes teaches GCSE, depending on how many pupils opt for it, but numbers have been rising since he and his head of department overhauled the Year 9 curriculum – he enjoys the flexibility of working in a non-NC subject. His current GCSE group is small but interested, although they lost a couple of potential A-grade students to history because the kids' parents insisted.

Each subject can argue why it experiences the best of times and the worst of times. So PE teachers will get the best out of the school's most notorious thug, and complain about having to lead cold and miserable after-school runs when everyone else has gone home, whereas English teachers are entrusted with poetry a child's parents will never be allowed to see, yet spend so many hours marking they rarely get time to read a novel themselves. The truth must be that no one has it easier, it's just that their experiences are different.

CASE STUDY

Cynog Dafis is a Plaid Cymru/Green MP, the first 'seat-share' in the House of Commons involving the Green Party. He taught Welsh and English in Pontardawe College of Further Education, and was Head of English at Newcastle Emlyn Secondary Modern, and at Aberaeron and Dyffryn Teifi Comprehensives. He next researched adult education at Swansea University, before winning his seat for Ceredigion and Pembrokeshire North in 1992. He is Plaid Cymru's spokesperson on the environment and agriculture, and parliamentary adviser to the NUT.

There are perhaps three elements about teaching which I treasure in retrospect and appreciated during the thirty-two years that I spent in the classroom. First is the personal relationship with the children. I was privileged to teach in a locality where the pupils by and large came from stable and loving backgrounds, and so they were well adjusted and friendly. This does not by any means mean that they were docile, but their liveliness was invariably innocent. It is a great joy now to meet former pupils who speak about their happy and fulfilling days at some of the schools where I taught.

The second factor is the immense satisfaction of teaching English literature for all that time. It meant that one was almost constantly in a state of emotional excitement and intellectual stimulation. Being able to arouse enthusiasm among pupils for fine literature was a great privilege. The third factor was the *esprit de corps* that one shared with fellow teachers.

My best career move was the decision to accept the post of an assistant teacher of English in a comprehensive after eighteen years of being head of department in an excellent secondary modern school. This involved a substantial drop in salary, but gave me my first opportunity to teach A level. I will never forget the joy of returning to the great classics and the satisfaction of mastering them sufficiently well to be able to teach them effectively.

WORKING WITH ADULTS

Teachers spend so much of their working life in the minority – a lone adult in the classroom – that it can be easy to forget their work in the adult sphere, although the skills used are much the same. Some of their most important contact with other adults is indirect, as they are in daily touch with parents through the pupils they teach. Their actions are constantly answerable to these crucial figures whom they may meet only once a year at a parents' evening, or once a fortnight whilst a child in their form group is experiencing a particular problem. Some recent developments have caused 'parent power' to be used and feared as a blunt instrument but, more usually, it's a tool to ensure the best interests of the child are met. Most schools see parents as their partners in the work of educating children; in practice, this means class teachers explaining their work and the child's progress clearly to parents, sometimes justifying themselves or standing up for the pupil, and most often drawing on invaluable home support. The same tact and respect is needed for the input of other interested parties – governors, primary colleagues, community figures – although responsibility for dealing with these groups is more usually in the hands of senior staff.

For the classroom teacher, working with adults generally means contact with other teachers in the school. Classroom teachers are team members, and, in the same way as there are three different types of teacher, there are three different types of colleague. As members of a department, they get together on subject business – anything from planning a scheme of lessons or tackling a problem with part of an exam syllabus, preparing materials for each other's use, establishing a policy on homework or cross-checking their marking, to doing their bit for the department's GCSE paperwork. In their year team, the general tasks are much the same, except now they are focused on the well-being, behaviour and general achievements of pupils in a year group – form tutors will get together with their year head to monitor attendance, look for ways of managing an outbreak of bullying, report back on individuals who need praise or a kick, or plan an end-of-year trip. As a staff member, the roles are combined as the teacher becomes part of a large pastoral and academic operation.

As with any team, you are expected to contribute ideas, respond to instructions, share in the work and decision-making, give feedback and keep to agreed goals. Much of this can involve meetings and paperwork (neither of which is high on teachers' wish lists of things to do at the end of a busy day when there are sixty unmarked exercise books waiting on the desk), but while it is a professional duty to keep in touch, working with colleagues on issues that matter can also be a pleasure. Planning a course of lessons with like-minded (or very different) thinkers can be an intellectual treat as well as a task halved; finding that you are not alone in your difficulties with 8K can keep you sane and effective next time you teach them; discussing the admission policy with a management team who are listening can renew your faith in your school. Teachers learn most from each other.

POUND SIGNS AND PROFESSIONAL PRIDE

In a 1996 NOP survey, members of the public were shown a list of ten professions, including doctors, lawyers, members of the emergency services, journalists, industrialists and financiers. 83 per cent saw teaching as being a 'rewarding profession'; 59 per cent ranked teachers as the professionals of most value to society, second only to doctors; and teaching was voted second highest, after medicine, in its potential for job satisfaction. The public's perception is right – teaching offers tremendous job satisfaction, whether in the instant hit of a good lesson or the long-term pleasure of seeing children reach their potential. As with many professions, especially those coming under the 'vocational' tag, the feeling that you are doing something which matters is one of its attractions. Although market forces have come decisively into schools, and there is now a prospect of scientific tests to determine a school's 'effectiveness', it is still a job where you can't measure success purely on a graph. The rewards of the job come in very personal forms, and one of the most commonly mentioned seems to be the feeling of worth associated with doing a good job, and being recognised for it. For many teachers, feeling valued and valuable scores higher on the scale of job satisfaction than financial returns. Another measure of success is the challenge the job continues to bring: 'If I am bored, I know it's time to move to a new post,' says a senior teacher and Head of Science, currently working as a staff development co-ordinator. And more simply, from a Head of Art after twenty-five years in teaching, 'Career success for me will be to end my career still with enthusiasm.'

Last and not least is the ordinary everyday job satisfaction, linked to good teaching, young people and their successes:

Lots of highs – writing, performing and directing plays; publishing magazines; running poetry groups; lessons that work perfectly; seeing light-bulbs go on over students' heads; exam results; stories or projects that seem like gifts; letters of appreciation; colleagues that work on the same wavelength.

Head of department, fifteen years in teaching

Meeting ex-pupils, now married with families . . . and 100 per cent turn-out to our Record of Achievement presentations, a most pleasant evening with over 600 in the hall.

Head of year, twenty-eight years in teaching

But is teaching rewarded, as well as rewarding? A sense of vocation can sit very happily next to the desire for a healthy bank balance, yet graduate teachers look to start work on a below-average salary, and remain in the lower band of graduate earnings over the next few years of employment. These salaries are determined by a points system, whereby teachers are awarded points according to qualifications, experience, and other criteria (see Appendix B for the official explanation of the points categories) and graduates usually start on point 2. The unions consistently complain about the lack of pay parity with other professionals. Judge for yourself; the current pay scales for classroom teachers (below head and deputy head level) are shown in Appendix B, but typically range from about £15,000 for a newly qualified to £35,000 at the top of the scale. Headteachers can earn as much as £59,000. You move up the scale annually, a point for every extra year in teaching, but to increase your income any quicker, you have to take on extra responsibilities and move into management.

It's the irony of many careers that the more you enjoy what you do and the better you get at the job, the more you are dragged away from it. Teachers will tell you their frustrations come from not having sufficient time to do the stuff that matters – talking to pupils, preparing great lessons, checking out new resources, sharing ideas with colleagues – and equally it has seemed that promotion is the only type of career progression to be valued and financially rewarded. For lots of teachers, moving up a management ladder holds no attractions, and the ability to 'get on' seems unconnected with excellent teaching. (This is why a head at a school publicised as 'successful' by Ofsted continues to spend one whole day a week teaching: 'To be seen to be a good teacher is an important part of my job. It's what gives credibility.') Experienced people, admired by colleagues and pupils, have found themselves at the top of the pay spine with no way of having their future improvement as teachers marked or rewarded; indeed the 1997 survey found that 50 per cent of all teachers are at the top of the class teachers' scale on points 9.9 to 13. What this means is that you could be an accomplished and experienced teacher of seven years' experience, yet still be on £21,000.

The good news is that this problem seems at last to be recognised, even if at this stage it's not solved. Anthea Millett, chief executive of the Teacher Training Agency, recently said:

If pay is not an important issue on day one of a teacher's career, it becomes important in the second or third years when teachers look round and see their friends buying better clothes and a better car; when they see that their own salary is not moving them forward in the way they would wish.

As the table shows, the DfEE have tried to ease the situation by making discretionary points (up to three) available for 'excellent teaching' and performance-related pay for teachers, heads and whole schools is being pushed increasingly in the political arena. At present, points can be awarded for the full range of a teacher's work – including outstanding contribution to extra-curricular activities – but are mainly designed to reward fine classroom teaching. However, the NASUWT says they are not being widely awarded. According to the union, this is because of the lack of money available to fund them, as so many class teachers would deserve them. Some heads consider them divisive because they can't award them as widely as they would like, and, crucially, there isn't always a fair and objective basis for their award.

However, there may soon be an agreed set of standards for excellent classroom teaching. The Teacher Training Agency is looking at the 'continuing professional development' of teachers throughout their careers; the agency is considering national qualifications, criteria and training to add up to a clearer career path. In terms of work in the classroom, one staging post (at least in terms of status) they are trying to define is the 'expert teacher'. This may or may not be the same as Labour's 'Advanced Skills Teacher', who is paid more to stay in the classroom, to act as a model for new teachers and others, and who would possibly link up with a higher-education trainer. This, in theory, fills the gap in the career structure for non-managers, but it remains to be seen how many teachers will be involved. David Blunkett has so far talked about only one advanced skills teacher per large school.

STAFF DEVELOPMENT AND TRAINING

If you don't change, you sink.
History teacher, twenty years in teaching

Teaching isn't a career where boredom is a major problem, but burn-out can be. Being in a classroom demands flexibility: 'You've got to react quickly to things, and think on your feet, as well as change for different classes – your pitch, speed of work, the level of help you give and the levels of participation or practical work,' says one old hand. 'You're also living with human change on a daily basis and seeing social trends slowly unfold. Children change, so this forces your development – you've got to react to their changing expectations of presentation, technology.' These demands aside, there are also external changes thrown at the profession. It's a very high-profile 'industry' so it isn't left alone for very long by any type of government – adapting to regular national policy reform is now a fact of life.

Coping with change isn't just down to the teacher's professionalism. Teachers' professional development is now on everyone's agenda, and a good thing too, after years of a rather patchy framework for developing and updating skills. The TTA has a unit working on teachers' development, and there's a lot of emphasis on creating a 'learning culture' for staff. It makes sense for a school to make sure that you, their employee, aren't stagnating – as a headteacher's bulletin on staff development says, 'In a nutshell, if the staff are learning, it is likely that the pupils are too.' The state of staff training is definitely an area worth looking at when you are considering whether to apply for a job in a new school; here are a number of schemes which already exist, some of which are statutory.

INSET

INSET stands for In-Service Training, and is the main way teachers refresh and extend their skills. Some INSET can be for a whole department and school, if you all need to work on common ground; there is also a budget for individual teachers' training. (Every school has a School Development Plan which sets out its goals in the foreseeable future, including what it needs to do in the way of staff development. If there's a new and compulsory government policy being introduced for, say, vocational qualifications, then staff will have to be trained; if the boys are lagging behind at GCSE in the school, it will want to look at techniques staff might use to stop the rot on an INSET day.) Some schools are – or are forced to be – very prescriptive in what they will pay for in the way of training, insisting on the most immediate relevance of the course to your work (for example, training only on statutory developments, or new syllabuses). Others can allow you a little more leeway to follow your interests and, importantly, career aspirations. Recent INSET is asked about on application forms, so keep a record of what you attend, and keep an eye out for suitable courses run by your LEA, teachers centre or consultants.

INSET is usually publicised in two ways: a general advertisement on a particular notice-board in the staffroom or, more helpfully, targeted by the person responsible for staff development, who would draw your attention to any courses running on an area you'd expressed an interest in, or which had come up in your appraisal or discussions with your line manager.

APPRAISAL

All schools are obliged to have a system of appraisal which helps teachers develop professionally, for the good of the teacher and the school. How effective these systems are varies in different schools although the Green Paper promises 'tough new arrangements' and links to pay. At present, appraisal is intended to develop the individual in a positive way. Each teacher is appraised on a two-yearly basis. In many schools you get to choose your appraiser, although often it's your line manager, and there should be discussion and a bit of give-and-take throughout the process.

You and your appraiser decide which areas of your work should be reviewed, according to your needs and the school's priorities. So, you might want to focus on the variety of your teaching with your sixth-form groups; the school might want all teachers to be improving their assessment techniques, so you'd add that too; and finally you might both agree that you should be getting some training in readiness for promotion in the next year or so. With this shopping list of skills and performance at the ready, your appraiser would then watch you at work in the classroom, or in a meeting, and if relevant speak to colleagues, looking precisely at those areas of your work. The report that came out of it would include plans for how your strengths and weaknesses could be built on, and what further training you need. This could simply take the form of more advice from colleagues, some time away from lessons to observe other teachers, or a more formal period of working with your head of department on your skills, support (moral, financial, or in the form of time) for extra study like an MA, or the traditional INSET.

INVESTORS IN PEOPLE

This is a national scheme to ensure that any company's staff development is of a high quality, and isn't specifically designed for schools. However, schools can get accredited if they meet the standards laid down in twenty-four 'Investors in People' criteria. In Croner's 'Bulletin for Headteachers', this is how the criteria were applied to schools:

Clearly a school which receives Investors in People accreditation and/or takes staff development seriously will:

- show a commitment from the top
- link staff development to the School Development Plan
- relate the programme of staff development to individual and whole-school needs
- set clear targets
- involve staff in the planning and delivery of development
- communicate the development opportunities available to staff
- ensure staff development is cost-effective and gets evaluated for its quality.

A school accredited by Investors in People is a good place to work: it probably indicates a head who is really committed to the progress of his or her staff, school planning which takes note that staff need to learn as well as children, and a well-organised system of publicising and organising courses and INSET which are beneficial to teachers as well as to the school. Look out for accreditation during job-hunting.

HOW TO STAY FRESH

So, as a teacher, some change you're born into, some change is achieved with time, and some change is thrust upon you. What you have to do and what you want to do to stay fresh are not always the same. But a recurrent piece of advice from experienced and happy teachers is that you get out what you put into the job. Self-development leads to job satisfaction and career success. Here are some ways of coping with or courting change. Try them for love, money or both ...

- ◆ *Use the school's systems of staff development: seek appraisal, INSET, or courses, give yourself a new goal.* 'Talk to people about what you want to do, and they'll usually help,' says one deputy head. Whether this support is in the way of time, training or mentors will depend on your school, but ask.

- ◆ *Join a subject association* (see Appendix A). These run conferences and discussion groups on subject areas, new developments and teaching, with national and often local wings. Your department might already have a group membership, so see what's already in school in the way of publications and publicity.

- *Enjoy the content of your lessons.* Plan lessons you like; get involved in curriculum development; work on a new syllabus, or choose new syllabus options if you can't change. 'Switching syllabus has been the single most important factor in my recent career. As a head of department, I wanted us to move to a course where we had more freedom to plan the work and fit it to our students. We voted as a department, and it's been great for everyone.'

- *Extend your pastoral role.* Maybe you're no longer as interested in what happens within the confines of your subject or classroom, and more concerned with the 'whole' child? Contact the National Association for Pastoral Care in Education for information about their training, conferences and journals, and career paths in this area.

- *Develop your subject or personal interests. Don't teach, do.* Stop reading essays and start reading around your subject, or learn something new yourself. Apply your subject in extra-curricular contexts – direct a play, start a poetry group, start a girls' football team, organise a gallery visit, lead a ski trip. Or use it in your own time – build a car, join a lacrosse team. Or get into some related employment: apply for moderating work with an exam board. Alternatively . . .

- *Get away from your subject.* Sign yourself up for a cross-curricular group on marking policy, or special needs, or IT. Volunteer to teach in a new subject area you are qualified in, or a general course like PSHE, or support teaching. Or set up a cross-curricular project with another department.

- *Get a qualification, applied or not.* 'My best career move was doing an MA in Science Education. It turned me from an ordinary science teacher into an excellent one!' A list of courses and where they are offered can be found in *Post-grad: The Directory of Graduate Studies*. Published by CRAC, this has a section on MAs and diplomas grouped under education subjects. It's also available on the Internet at www.hobsons.co.uk.

- *Evaluate yourself.* See where you fall on David Berliner's expert scale, which can, apparently, be applied to experts in all fields – the air traffic controller, physicist or chess player. In the Open University book of essays on *Teaching and Learning in the Secondary School*, Berliner plots five stages on the road to gurudom. Roughly paraphrased, they go as follows for teaching:

Stage 1: The Novice
Typical years in teaching: 0–1
What you've got: verbal knowledge – theory, a list of tasks, some new jargon (like 'reinforcement') and 'context-free' rules you've learnt at teaching college. So come hell or high water, you 'don't smile till Christmas' and 'never criticise a student'. Every move is thought out, and you don't deviate from your lesson plan.
What you need: more experience.

Stage 2: Advanced Beginner
Typical years in teaching: 2–3
What you've got: verbal knowledge and experience. You've seen some situations more than once and carry over what you've learnt, and your rules are now becoming more 'strategic' – you're ready to hold off with the praise for another lesson lest your top group get smug. But you're probably still not able to see the wood for the trees, and are following the rules rather than making them.
What you need: to do your own thing.

Stage 3: Competent
Years in teaching: 3–4 years with motivation; may take longer without.
What you've got: priorities, plans and sensible means of

achieving them. A sense of what's important and what's not, and when to time an activity, ignore a remark or move on to a new topic. You're following your own lead and reacting to the context of your actual class, school or teaching slot. You feel responsible for what happens in your classroom, and have intense feelings and memories of your successes and failures.

What you need: to get faster, more fluent and more flexible.

Stage 4: Proficient
Years in teaching: 5 minimum, but only a modest number of individuals reach this stage.

What you've got: a growing sixth sense about why things happen and how to deal with them. Muscle memory is coming into play, like changing gear in the car without thinking. You see situations as a whole, without having to dissect them into categories. You make holistic connections – for example, between the qualities of good lessons – and you can predict how a teaching or discipline situation will go precisely. But your decision making is still analytical. You are like the tournament chess and bridge players; you haven't quite made it to grand master.

What you need: that extra something.

Stage 5: Expert
Years in teaching: hard to tell, but you will be one of only a small number of proficients to graduate.

What you've got: 'Arationality'. You are so good you don't usually have to think about the job – you say exactly the right thing, give exactly the right mark, choose exactly the right activity without being aware you are doing it. Your routines and systems work fluently and your pace is brisk. You often get the feeling your lesson moved along so beautifully you never had to teach it. Yours is knowledge in action, poetry in motion – so when something goes wrong (which it hardly ever does) you are deeply upset.

What you need: a medal.

Breaking In

GETTING A TASTER

Everyone's been to school, so everyone thinks they know what being a teacher involves. However, the reality may be different, and it's worth finding that out before you begin applying for courses. The message from all sources is to start your homework early; training courses fill up quickly and last-minute applications are less and less likely to be successful. This applies especially to candidates who are restricted to certain colleges or routes because of their subject specialism, or perhaps because they can't travel or relocate for their training. It's also especially important for anyone who thinks they might have difficulties over entry requirements. So start investigations early.

Absolutely the best way to start is to get yourself into a school for a close look at the job. A personal contact is the easiest way; your local head may also be amenable to you coming in and shadowing a member of staff for a day, or you could contact your LEA to see if they can offer a taster course, often funded by the TTA, or suggest an approachable school. If means allow, an extended trial is the cast-iron way of making sure you aren't wasting your time: before applying for her PGCE, one civil servant negotiated a four-day week contract for a period, and went to work in her local secondary as a voluntary assistant. If you have a teacher training college close to you, they may be able to offer you a taster course also. You don't have to be in a teaching role to work with children, of course. Any kind of paid or voluntary youth work – a summer playgroup job, or involvement in a club – will give you an idea of whether you'd be happy spending your working life with young people, and whether you're suited to it.

Work experience or shadowing isn't just a good idea for the undecided. If you know teaching is for you, it will also be a way of persuading teacher trainers that you're serious and suitable for a place on their course; there's a section on the GTTR application form (see below) which asks you to write about your relevant work with children and visits to schools. And lastly, it will be useful for your CV when – or if – you get to applying for your first job.

You'll be especially welcomed by the profession if you are interested in teaching one of the 'priority' shortage subjects: science, maths, information and design technology, modern languages, religious studies, physical education and, in Wales, Welsh. There are all sorts of efforts being made to get suitably qualified people in these areas into teaching, so don't assume you are too old, or that your experience doesn't fit, or that you can't get trained, without making enquiries first. Disabled people should, can and do work in teaching. If you are disabled and your appointment would require a school to make changes to the workplace, there are plenty of sources of assistance. Unions give the teacher and the head advice on how to proceed and which organisations to contact. Job centres have Placing, Assessment and Counselling Teams (PACTs) administering the national Access to Work Scheme, and advising on facilities for disabled workers. Many adjustments to the workplace cost next to nothing, but this scheme is well resourced, and can pay for adaptations to equipment or premises and travel expenses for employees. Teachers with disabilities can also write to the Department of Health (PO Box 410, Wetherby LS23 7LN) for its information on services and equipment published in *A Practical Guide for Disabled People*, to RADAR, and to other charitable organisations dealing with their specific disability (see a selection of contacts in Appendix A).

The profession also desperately needs more teachers from the ethnic minorities. The teaching force in Britain is in no way representative of our multiracial society, which means that children aren't getting a balanced range of role models, and teaching talent in the ethnic communities is going to waste. The reasons for this under-representation aren't fully understood by the Teacher Training Agency, which says the issue is complex. Teaching may have an image problem in some ethnic communities, to compound difficulties with access, which is why the Agency is holding multi-ethnic conferences, and why it already funds taster courses aimed specifically at ethnic communities. Mentoring schemes are also being discussed. Whatever the case, not enough would-be teachers from ethnic minorities are getting onto the training courses they are applying for (with some exceptions, like the Universities of North London and Wolverhampton) and everyone is keen for this to change. Follow the advice below for general information. If you are an aspiring teacher and would like support and information specifically for people from the ethnic minorities, contact your local authority, teachers' centre and your union to find out what is available in your local area. For example, there are black and Asian teachers' groups at present in the London boroughs of East London, Harrow, Lewisham and Waltham Forest, in Ipswich, in Coventry, in Berkshire, Nottinghamshire and Milton Keynes; there may also be a more informal network you can tap into.

GETTING QUALIFIED

To work in any maintained secondary school, you will first need to be properly qualified with QTS (qualified teaching status). The only exceptions to this are when you are embarking on an on-the-job training scheme which leads to a qualification, or some jobs in independent schools.

Once you have attained QTS, you can get on with applying for a secondary-level job. With your QTS comes a certificate, a teacher number and, from your course, a profile. This profile, new from the summer of 1997, details NQTs' competencies and strengths, and will be the basis of your further training at your first school. The induction year for new teachers is being reinstated and you will become a fully fledged member of the profession having completed it.

Your main general sources of information on the best route to getting qualified should be:

- Teacher Training Agency (Information Line on 01245 454454), for general info on the profession and training. They publish *Routes into Teaching*, a guide to courses and qualifications in England and Wales, and other useful handouts listed in Appendix A; all these are available from their Communication Centre (PO Box 3210, Chelmsford, Essex CM1 3WA, telephone as Information Line above, fax 01245 261668).

- Teacher Education Admissions Clearing House (TEACH), for information on teacher training in Scotland. Write to PO Box 165, Edinburgh EH8 8AT (0131 558 6169/70) for an information pack called 'Teaching in Scotland'.

- To train to teach in Northern Ireland, contact DENI, at Department of Education, Teachers Branch, Waterside, 75 Duke Street, Londonderry BT47 1FP (01504 319000).

You'll obviously want to find the route which is right for your experience and circumstances. Here's an overview of what is available:

'I'VE ALREADY GOT A DEGREE, AND I KNOW WHAT SUBJECT I WANT TO TEACH'

Far and away the most common route is the year-long full-time training course which follows your degree course, namely the PGCE (Postgraduate Certificate in Education). Teacher training colleges and university departments offering this qualification are listed in the GTTR handbook, which is updated annually; you will need to check that they run courses in your chosen subject specialism and the 11–18 age group.

The other recent addition to the full-time route is via SCITT (School-centred Initial Teacher Training), where students train not at a college or university but with a group of schools. PGCEs are available with some ITT colleges on a part-time basis over two years, and the Open University offers a distance learning course over eighteen months.

To get onto a PGCE course, you are usually expected to hold a degree in the subject you want to teach, but the training colleges will look at graduates whose degree subject overlaps with a school subject (for example engineering and maths). The decision whether to admit you is down to them. You also need GCSEs in maths and English, at a minimum of a C grade, or an equivalent. You should contact the training college you are interested in, to see whether you have the right entry qualifications (or how you might satisfy them). You will need to declare yourself physically fit to teach – aspiring teachers who are disabled should contact a college for information on how this affects them. Two other useful organisations are RADAR – the Royal Association for Disability and Rehabilitation – who publish 'So You Want to be a Teacher: Guidelines for Entry into Teaching for the Disabled', and SKILL (the National Bureau for Students with Disability). The Open University publishes 'School Experience in the Open University PGCE: A guide for disabled students'. Finally, you must declare any criminal convictions, which the training college will advise you about.

The PGCE covers the teaching of your particular subject, and teaching in general. Lectures and seminars at college will cover aspects like the National Curriculum requirements, methods of teaching important for your subject, exam courses, assessment and reporting, classroom management, planning, teaching different abilities, pastoral issues and teachers' legal liabilities (relating to health and safety, child protection and so on). Teacher training itself has acquired its own 'national curriculum' which all trainers must deliver: there is now a greater emphasis on teacher expectations of pupils, knowledge of the special educational needs code of practice, and of how information technology can be used in their subject. Over the years, the course has become more practical, with two lengthy blocks (twenty-four weeks) of actual teaching in two different schools, and additional days spent observing and researching in school. Teaching practice puts all you've heard about and discussed into action, and gives you some real experience to inform your studies at college. You are assigned a mentor at your teaching practice school who advises you, observes your teaching and gives you feedback on how you are doing; a tutor from college will also monitor your progress. You are continually assessed, both on your work at college – projects and essays – and your performance on teaching practice.

LEAs give grants for the year's course, to cover course fees and maintenance grants (if applicable). Information on grants is given in the DfEE booklet 'Student grants and loans – a brief guide for higher education students', available from the DfEE or your LEA. For Scotland, there's 'A Guide to Student Allowances' (published by the Scottish Office Education Department), and 'Student Grants and Loans: A Brief Guide' from the Department of Education for Northern Ireland, which is available from the department or your local education and library board. You should contact your LEA's Awards section to see precisely what you are eligible for in terms of funding. There are also additional national funds for the shortage subjects. The money is used differently by different training institutions, so contact the college – grants may be in the shape of payments for experience, on hardship grounds, to fund attachments or travel.

'I'VE GOT A DEGREE, BUT NOT IN THE SUBJECT I WANT TO TEACH'

Conversion PGCEs are available for shortage subjects – Chemistry, Craft Design and Technology, Mathematics, Modern Languages, Physics or Science. They last two years, and may give you a diploma in the subject, as well as a teaching qualification. Your first degree will need to have included at least one year of study which is relevant to the subject you want to switch to. See above for additional funding for priority subjects.

'I DON'T HAVE A DEGREE'

There are degree courses which include teacher training. Bachelor of Education degrees (B.Eds) are mainly taken by primary teachers, but there are some secondary B.Ed. courses on offer in a few subjects. An alternative is a Bachelor of Arts or Science combined with teaching (BA or B.Sc. with QTS). For mature entrants who have a suitable level of knowledge in a degree subject (for example an HND), there is a shortened B.Ed. course on offer.

Most degree courses will require a minimum of two A levels in relevant subjects, and the equivalent to C grade GCSEs in English and Maths. BTEC nationals may also fit the bill, but this will need to be checked. If you've had a less standard educational experience, however, you might find an Access course is what you need, to enable you to move into higher education. These run at lots of FE colleges, and are generally more flexible in their hours and facilities. You'll need to be at least twenty, and you may be able to get a means-tested grant from your LEA. Contact your local college to see what courses they have, or for a full list of providers, ask for an Access to Higher Education Courses Directory from ECCTIS, PO Box 88, Walton Hall, Milton Keynes MK7 6DB. Recognised courses are also listed in a handout from the Access Courses Recognition Group, Higher Education Quality Council, 344–354 Grays Inn Road, London WC1X 8BP (0171 837 2223).

'I WANT TO TRAIN ON THE JOB'

In independent schools, this can happen without much fuss; the schools do recruit unqualified graduates, many of whom then go on to achieve QTS through a distance learning course. In the state sector, it's unusual but possible, and the route taken primarily by mature entrants. The two options are the Licensed Teacher Scheme (course length depending on what you've done before and offered by individual schools) or the Registered Teacher Scheme running only in CTCs (with a science technology bias); information about these is available from the address in Appendix A. But watch this space. The White Paper seems to be promising a new (but widely scoffed-at) fast-track employment-based route of two terms. There will also be new regulations on on-the-job training from autumn 1997, so contact the TTA as your starting point.

'I'M ALREADY A TRAINED TEACHER – BUT WASN'T TRAINED IN THE COUNTRY WHERE I WANT TO WORK'

It may be that you won't have to undertake any further training at all. Contact the DfEE Teachers Qualifications Team (01325 392120/1/2/3) if you are a teacher trained in Scotland, Northern Ireland or Europe, and want to know whether you have recognised qualifications to teach in England or Wales. If you want to move into a Scottish school, you should contact the General Teaching Council for Scotland as only teachers registered with them are eligible to teach in Scotland. For requirements to teach in Northern Ireland, see the leaflet 'To be a teacher', from DENI, mentioned above.

If you're a teacher trained outside the EU, then it's unlikely your qualifications will be recognised immediately. (Teachers from Norway, Liechtenstein and Iceland are the exception.) Contact the DfEE Labour Service to discuss your situation and work permits. You can achieve QTS through on-the-job training, however, if you can first secure employment in a school – the Overseas Trained Teacher Scheme, the Licensed Scheme or Registered Teacher Scheme are all possibilities (although the Overseas Scheme is specifically designed as an introduction to teaching content and methods in England and Wales). The address of the information source on these courses is listed in Appendix A.

COURSES

Once you've chosen your route, the rest of your information should come from individual institutions. The *Handbook of Initial Teacher Training* (published by NAFTHE), available in careers and public libraries, lists what courses are available and where. Alternatively you can use the ECCTIS 2000 database. The individual training college(s) or provider(s) will then be able to give you detailed information on courses and entry requirements. Check the fine details of courses with the training college or provider by speaking to an admissions tutor and reading a prospectus. Things to consider will be the course content, possible subject combinations, the entry requirements and whether you are eligible, what sort of teaching practice is available, as well as your own personal considerations (like college locations, size, accommodation, facilities and social life). Then you can draw up a short list of places you want to apply to. You are allowed to apply to up to four institutions at a time, and you will need to put your choices in order of preference.

MAKING YOUR TRAINING APPLICATIONS

To follow a degree course of teacher education, go through the University and College Admissions Service (UCAS) in the normal way for degree courses. Speak to your school careers officer, or local careers office; these will have UCAS handbooks and college prospectuses. Or write direct to UCAS for this information.

Applications for postgraduate training in England and Wales are made through the GTTR (Graduate Teacher Training Registry). Get an application form from them in the autumn – copies are available from mid-September of the year before you want to begin your course. (Deferred entry applications aren't allowed except by special agreement with a college.) There is no closing date for applications, but all the advice is to get in early, as the GTTR send off candidates' details to colleges on a first-come, first-served basis. If you delay, there may not be spaces left in your chosen institutions. The GTTR usually begin contacting course providers in early November.

The GTTR sends off your details to your chosen colleges one by one, starting with your first choice, who will decide whether they want to interview you. This process continues until one of your colleges writes to the GTTR to tell them you've been given a place. If you exhaust your initial four choices – either because there are no vacancies left on the course, or because you are rejected – you can apply to other course providers who still have vacancies.

If you have questions about how to apply, you can phone the GTTR helpline on 01242 544788. Remember that the GTTR only handle the application process – they don't make decisions about who gets places. Any course queries should go to the admissions tutor of the college concerned.

Applications for Scottish and Northern Irish postgraduate teaching courses are arranged through the following bodies, not the GTTR. For Scotland, application forms come from TEACH, PO Box 165, Edinburgh EH8 8AT, and need to be submitted by mid-December. In Northern Ireland, contact the Department of Education for Northern Ireland, Rathgael House, Balloo Road, Bangor, Co. Down BT19 2BR (01504 319000).

COURSE INTERVIEWS

As with any interview, you'll need to look at your application form and be ready to expand on what's there. Expect the obvious questions – why you want to teach, why this age group, your own subject enthusiasms, past experience with youth work and what you know about teaching from school visits. The interviewers will be interested in your personal qualities and skills, so if you've worked before, you will be able to talk about the qualities you showed in the workplace, or if you're straight from college, you might want to talk about involvement in the life of your school or HE institution, personal achievements, summer jobs, or the way you approached certain academic tasks.

You won't need to know the national curriculum and syllabuses for your subject off by heart, but it makes sense to be up to date with the work of teachers and pupils, and general education issues. School visits will help you to be aware what sort of work is going on in your subject at Key Stage 3, GCSE and post-16. Try also to talk to a teacher or two about the wider role for teachers and schools in preparing pupils for adult life. You can also dip into the education press (The *TES* on Friday, *Guardian* on Tuesday, *Independent* and *Telegraph* on Thursday and *The Times* on Monday). TASC publish a helpful little leaflet on what to expect and how to prepare for a teacher training interview, available from their publicity unit.

THE COURSE

Make the most of it is the best piece of advice. Here's your chance to immerse yourself in teaching theory and practice, with none of the distractions which will follow the moment you get a permanent job. One teacher trainer says: 'Experiment. Obviously you want to do well on your teaching practices – and it's important that you do – but this is the time to see what works for you. You may not feel in a position to take risks once you are working full time. And whilst it's good that the course offers practical experience, this is also your opportunity to be very reflective on what teaching is all about.'

A good read to accompany your training year – or as another way of testing the water – is *Learning to Teach in the Secondary School*. This is written by three teacher-trainers – from Canterbury, Leicester and London – and is published by Routledge.

Deborah Gallagher has just finished a PGCE in Modern Foreign Languages. She says the course content covered all you'd expect and need:

The teaching of modern languages, National subject matter, levels, differentiation, language teaching strategies, GCSE and A level, textbooks used, special projects, IT, pupils with special educational needs and classroom management skills.

She did emphasise however that the delivery of this content was most useful when it came through outside speakers:

The course cohort was quite small and we had two regular course teachers. It was therefore very refreshing to hear new voices and new angles, beyond the views of our tutors. We had another tutor from a PGCE course in Bath, a sixth-form teacher, a teacher from an inner-city school with severe discipline problems, and their talks were like a breath of fresh air.

Her move to teaching came after a first career, although

I had always wanted to teach. However, I'm from Northern Ireland, and on graduation from Aberystwyth, my LEA would initially only fund me for teacher training if I returned home. I was rejected at interview as I'd done my first degree outside Northern Ireland, so I spent my next years in administration and management. I found it too boring for words and decided to reapply for teaching, still in England. This time, I got my place on a relatively new course in my chosen subject – Modern Foreign Languages but with minimal French – in the college down the road. The subject and place, and the fact the course was small, were the reasons I chose my college.

Teaching is very different from my previous career – my last post was a job in the sense that when I left at 5 p.m., that was the end of my day. Teaching is more a way of life (and you can get very boring about it!). But it was helpful having been in business administration. I had IT and general organisational skills. This meant I could make attractive teaching materials, set up workable assessment and monitoring sheets and so on.

Having done the course, I now know teaching is for me, although I had some doubts on my first block practice. I don't have any concrete ideas on the actual shape that I want my career to take and in this uncertain age I feel it would be unwise to have my plans engraved on tablets of stone. But I do know I have two options – to follow subject interest, going through the second-in-command line to developing subject policy and schemes of work, and eventually becoming head of department. Or perhaps a management role on the pastoral side. It really depends on what is available at the school. Career advice was a bit weak on my course – we had a brief talk from a local headteacher, one day of mock interviews and a pep talk from our tutors assuring us we'd get a job. The main advice was always 'Keep looking in the *TES*.'

I have a job, but it wasn't what I set out to look for. Initially, I decided not to look at the type of school I had done my teaching practice in – low attainment and discipline were problems. I talked to friends teaching locally about which schools had good reputations, staff and results, and that was helpful. I looked initially for jobs in my area, and also

Catholic schools. I eventually got a job which was perfect for me but not in my area – I'll have a long journey or I'll have to move. The post is at a CTC, which is independently funded by business, but offers free education to pupils who live locally and who have expressed an interest – not necessarily an ability – in technology. The school is wonderfully resourced with a special focus on technology, so it has a wealth of computers and a state-of-the-art Sony languages lab! This is wonderful. All schools should be like this, but in my practice I found the lack of resources to be the single most significant factor in lack of motivation and learning.

This post also offers me an additional allowance because of a longer school day, and say what I might about teaching being vocational, we are all motivated by money. My age and previous business experience were taken into account, and merited accordingly.

GETTING A JOB

Friday is *TES* day, the weekly publication date for the source of teaching jobs which are externally advertised. Posts are advertised elsewhere – look in Tuesday's 'Education' *Guardian*, religious newspapers like the *Church Times* or *Jewish Chronicle* for the voluntary-aided denominational schools, and specialist publications mentioned in chapter 6 for jobs abroad, and the TTA website if you have access to the Internet – but the *Times Educational Supplement* is a central, reliable source of what employment is being offered in education. It has sections covering secondary jobs at all levels and in all subjects, special education and independent secondary schools. It also covers related employment, for example EFL appointments, LEA and tutoring posts and examination work. You can also access the paper (and related education information) on the Internet at http://www.tes.co.uk.

Other sources of information about jobs are varied. Local authorities have vacancy lists, so if you know what geographical areas you are interested in, contact them for mailings. Some LEAs operate pool systems, where you can apply centrally and your CV is sent to local schools, but this is not as widespread as in primary recruitment. Teacher trainers are often able to give their students tips on local jobs and the quality of the schools which are advertising; LEA advisers can do the same for teachers already in post. Head-hunting goes on occasionally, too.

Teacher recruitment – because it's based around academic years and terms – operates on a musical-chairs basis, as teachers move schools and posts simultaneously in the run up to resignation dates. Deadlines for notice are:

> 31 October (if you want to leave at Christmas, or the end of the autumn term)

> 28 February (if you want to leave at Easter, or the end of the spring term)

> 31 May (if you want to leave at the end of the summer term)

The job market is at its height between March and May, when recruitment is taking place for September; for NQTs, the summer round may be more extended as they aren't in a chain or tied by notice deadlines. There is another little flurry from September as posts for January onwards come up. (Posts are advertised throughout the year of course due to maternity leaves, sickness, retirement and general resignations, but in far fewer numbers.)

FIRST JOB, FIRST SCHOOL

Everyone has to start somewhere. Your first job is an important one, as you will want a positive experience to send you on your way. As discussed in chapter 3, your idea of a positive experience might be another NQT's poison, but teaching practice and your PGCE year as a whole should have helped you clarify what sort of schools you want to teach in or avoid. Whatever your preferences, it might be sensible to keep your options open at this stage, and avoid limiting yourself to a school which is too distinctive – a selective boys' school may not be the best springboard from which to launch your career. A deputy in charge of appointments says: 'I've seen hundreds of application forms and interviewed many teachers. I would say that single-sex, or 16–18, or selective experiences go against candidates if you don't know if they can manage the rest – the younger students, or the less able or motivated. It's also something I ask student teachers if their teaching practice schools are very similar.' Also avoid those few schools where you'll be so busy breaking up fights that you won't get a chance to deliver your lessons, and will be burnt out by the end of your first term.

Make yourself a shopping list before you open the job pages, even if this results in a pledge to look for the standard comprehensive. You may have to compromise, but it will help your trawl through the adverts. Look at chapter 3 for general information about choosing a school. The unions often publish good guides for NQTs – for example the NUT's 'Obtaining your first teaching post' looks at applications, interviews, contracts and pay. The *TES* usually publishes a supplement at the beginning of the spring term (around January), looking at First Appointments, packed with articles and advice from teachers and trainers. Finally, there's the sister book to *Learning to Teach* mentioned above, called *Starting to Teach in Secondary School.* Also published by Routledge, it covers the transition from student teacher to NQT, improving your teaching, working with your school mentor, teamwork and other useful areas and may give you some ideas on what you are looking for.

Crucially, you want somewhere which will support you as an NQT; it's a challenging time and with the formal probationary year gone at present, you need to be sure that the school is sensitive to your needs and willing to watch over you. Many posts are advertised as being 'suitable for an NQT', so you may be told about INSET in the job information the school sends you; if not, make sure you find out at interview how they will help you settle into your new career. The NUT says it is good practice for schools and LEAs to include the following in their arrangements for new teachers:

- a nominated member of staff to give you regular support and guidance, e.g. a senior teacher
- regular observation opportunities, both of experienced staff at work in class, and of neighbouring schools

- meetings with other new teachers, in the school and local area
- some guaranteed non-contact time for planning, preparation and advice-seeking
- systems for advice and feedback to NQTs
- an informal meeting with the governing body.

The application process for NQTs is more or less the same as for other teachers. The only real difference is that your application and interview will be based on more limited experience. You will draw more heavily on your teaching practice experience than you're ever likely to again, and on what you were doing before you switched to teaching. Make sure you think about useful experience, skills and qualities you can point to in your previous career, school and HE life, and interests. It helps to be able to show experience of teamwork, leadership qualities, activity and interest in your subject area, and communication skills.

INTERNAL APPLICATIONS

The first and most obvious place to look for a new challenge is on your own doorstep. (See chapter 4 on some of the pitfalls of internal promotion, though.) You are also much more likely to be given a chance in a new area, one where you are possibly untried and untested, on the strength of your general record and attitude: 'I would never have got this far this quickly if Mr Roberts, my head, hadn't believed in me,' says one young pastoral head, who was entrusted with a deputy pastoral role and then confirmed in her Acting Head of Year role within the space of a year.

There are other good reasons for staying put in your school if you are happy there. Certain types of jobs or roles within a school are less likely to be advertised externally, particularly 'acting' jobs where you cover a more senior member of staff and those attracting single responsibility points. Not for nothing were responsibility points once called incentive allowances. Heads can use them to offer career progression, recognition and encouragement to existing members of staff, and they are far less likely to be attached permanently to a specific post. Single points can also be used to fund the work of teachers taking on projects specific to the school, possibly for a limited period or to cover certain responsibilities at departmental level.

Internal promotion should not, of course, mean deals in dark corners. There should be a proper process of advertising and interviewing for all posts, announcements in staff briefings and departmental meetings. If you need encouragement and advice on what to apply for, go and see your line manager, or the deputy in charge of staff, or anyone you trust as a sounding board.

It's probably true to say that it's easy to underestimate the formality of internal advertising and interviewing. 'I didn't do myself justice because I expected a quick chat about the work everyone knew I was doing. I got the job anyway because of my track record, but it was embarrassing!' said an art teacher of her interview for temporary deputy in her department. So whilst you may not want to draw wry staffroom comments by wearing your very best power suit on the day of an internal interview, it pays to be properly prepared for what will happen behind closed doors and prepare as you would for an external interview.

Even if there's no formal post in the offing, jobs can come if you are proactive – go to see your head of department or alliance or even your headteacher to discuss openings for new responsibilities. Responsibilities taken on voluntarily often turn into tasks considered worthy of a point – see chapters 1 and 4 – especially with a supportive curriculum manager or head of year lobbying for you.

EXTERNAL APPLICATIONS

Schools are relatively small organisations, and even if you are ready for promotion, there may not be space for you to move up the ladder or take on a new role. This is why people move schools, coupled with the need to try somewhere new and broaden their experience. It's also why people take a sideways move – same job but different school. This can be very helpful, if you do your homework carefully and check that the move will give you the change you need. Being a Head of Maths or deputy head somewhere new will alter your experience of the job if, for example, achievement is much lower or higher, there's a significant shift in school ethos or size, or the school is working on a change which interests you. And there may be more of a chance of promotion in your new situation.

APPLICATIONS

The advert will tell you what's required – a letter and CV, or a completed application form supplied by the school. Make sure you check closing dates carefully. As resignation dates loom in late May, things become notoriously rushed – one teacher learnt of her interview by fax at 5 o'clock the day before – so contact the school for post details and forms immediately. Have a draft CV ready on a word processor or notepad, so you're not scrabbling round trying to find out exactly when you did your A levels and the address of your last school when the application materials arrive.

Once you've received the school's information and decided you want to apply (see chapter 3 for issues to consider), make sure your application is tailored to the post. A focused and clear covering letter or statement is what is required; keep it to the point. Some sections of your letters and forms will be much the same whoever you apply to, but emphasise the aspects of your experience which are most relevant – put them first in your letter or statement, or go into them in more detail. Try to match what you've done to the job description, and look carefully at a person specification if there is one. Some post details split into 'essential' and 'desirable' – make sure you structure your response accordingly. Hard evidence of your skills and qualities is more impressive than vague assurances alone that you are 'excellent' or 'caring'; it's better to find some objective way of showing this, or to let your referees make these kind of judgements. You may, however, be asked to outline your 'philosophy of education' or approach to teaching, and can be a little more abstract here (but have examples to back up your opinions ready for interview).

Check your application carefully before sending it off – teachers are supposed to be able to communicate, and this includes being able to write to a decent standard. If you can't get the spelling right here, you won't inspire short-listers with much confidence that you will communicate accurately and clearly on school reports or pupils' work. (One head of science was overheard saying: 'We've got to interview this one. With spelling like this, she'll have a great sense of humour – great to work with', but that's rather an idiosyncratic approach!) Finally, take a copy – you'll probably be making lots of applications at the same time, so you can't expect to remember what aspects of your experience you emphasised in which application.

INTERVIEWS

Teaching interviews are very public affairs. Candidates are usually invited to attend at the same time, and if you are pursuing a job in a particular area or at a particular level, you may find yourself making new friends as the same faces reappear on your interview days! This can be embarrassing if, for example, you are competing with a colleague or fellow student teacher, but more positively it can be reassuring to share first impressions.

Expect to be looked over by a great many people. As teaching is such a people-oriented field, you will invariably meet the team or department in which the job is going, and their views are often canvassed, so be nice to everyone! It's helpful to get a sense of the people on the staff and the dynamics of the department and it's worth keeping alert to what you might learn about general relations, working atmosphere, priorities and sociability. You may also get a chance to talk to teachers in more depth while waiting for your interview, and it can pay to make the most of the opportunity to gather information and opinions about the school.

The process will usually start with a tour of the school, often with the post-holder or someone involved in selection. This is the ideal way to get a feel for the school. You will be told a lot, but keep looking too – at how pupils behave, teachers at work, notice-boards, resources, rooms and the work on display. (One teacher going for a pastoral promotion made a point of finding out when classes or break started at the schools where she was to be interviewed, and turned up early 'to stand at the school gates and just watch the kids going in'.) There can be an unseemly rush to ask 'intelligent questions' on these tours; obviously you will want to show you are interested and, more importantly, you will want to find out certain key pieces of information, but don't feel you have to engage in some competition for the most obscure fact. Concentrate on finding out what's important to you, and listen to what you are being told – it will probably show you what's considered important in the school. Thereafter, you will probably spend time in the staffroom or department, followed by a long and rather tedious wait with the other candidates whilst you are all interviewed.

Interviews are usually taken by a three- or four-strong panel, consisting of some combination of the head, a deputy, the head of department, a governor or LEA officer, and it's important to be responsive to them all. At most teaching levels, you will be asked a combination of practice and principle questions. The panel want to find out what sort of teacher you are, as well as whether you fit the bill in terms of experience and your CV so far, so expect a range of areas to be covered:

- ♦ Could you give us an example of a lesson where you were successful in meeting the needs of the most able?
- ♦ What relevant experience do you have for this promoted post?
- ♦ What do you get out of teaching?
- ♦ What could you offer to the wider life of the school?
- ♦ How have you managed a change in policy or practice in your current post of responsibility?
- ♦ What makes a good pastoral deputy?
- ♦ Which historical period/current scientific debate are you most interested in?

- Which area of the National Curriculum do you think presents the greatest teaching challenge?

- What would you do with a child who refused to do homework?

In preparation, it is obviously crucial to make sure that you've thought about why your experience and skills fit you for the post. It's sometimes easy to get bogged down in what sound like meaningless and corny clichés when you're preparing. Speeches on what George Bush memorably called 'the vision thing' often flow better in the heat of the moment when you are feeling less self-conscious, so a more useful exercise is to break down your past and current jobs into tasks and responsibilities and achievements, however minor. Having those concrete examples at your fingertips can give you confidence, and you can then edit out anything which looks trivial. In short, go through the same process as you did with your application.

Your own career intentions, recent successes, enthusiasms and 'learning experiences' are also good areas to rehearse. In interview for posts of responsibility, the panel often wants to know where you see yourself going in career terms: 'I'm surprised at how coy people are. I want to know what ambitions people have, and that they've thought at least a few years ahead,' says one regular interviewer. Practise thinking about how you would deal with hypothetical management situations likely to arise in the job or school – how you would deal with an uncooperative colleague or an anxious parent. You should run through your skills in working with colleagues as well as pupils, and especially where the post is at managerial level, think about developments in education policy relevant to the post or school. One would-be deputy head of department was told he had not got the post because 'it's obvious you only read the *TES* for the job pages'!

You may be given specific preparation or tasks to do, although this usually happens at managerial level. You may be asked to teach a lesson (to the panel or a real class), give a presentation on a pressing issue at the school, sort and prioritise an in-tray, write a paper on how to implement an idea, chair a meeting or participate in a joint planning exercise.

Somewhere in the interview and usually at the end, you will be asked whether you are still a serious candidate for the job, and given a chance to ask questions. As with any career, there are obvious areas to avoid – for example, don't ask questions which give the impression you are interested in the job purely because of geographical convenience or money. Clear up any confusions which remain about the duties, terms and conditions involved and do ask about anything which is especially important to you ('Will I get a chance to be involved in school sports?'), but don't be afraid to pass if you already know all you need to know.

Many schools then ask you to wait until all interviews are over and a decision has been made, after which a member of the panel usually appears and invites 'Mrs X' to step outside to be offered the job. This is not the best way of breaking it to you gently if you are unsuccessful, but bizarre though they are in this respect, teaching interviews do have the advantage of being wrapped up in one go, and you won't have the delay of hearing by post. (A kinder tactic is where you are allowed to go home and a phone call that evening lets you know the result.) It also concentrates the mind – having to decide whether you want the job and whether to accept it on the day sharpens your antennae and, curiously, it is usually easy to tell whether this is the place for you. Also, if the teacher who is eventually offered the job refuses it (perhaps because they can't agree on the nitty gritty), the school can then turn to their next choice without delay.

The real difficulty with this wham-bam approach is when a teacher has a number of interviews to attend. This particularly affects NQTs who make a lot of applications in a short space of time when trying for their first job. You might feel quite happy with the job you are offered on Tuesday but know you have an interview with the school of your dreams on Wednesday. It is possible to ask a school to hold an offer but they may want to appoint there and then, or feel you should want them as desperately as they do you. It is considered deeply unprofessional to accept on the day but then renege on your decision, and if you do so, your behaviour may be publicised and come back to haunt you. But if your bargaining power is strong, you may be able to choose – one NQT was driven by the head of a school to her next interview, so he could have more time to persuade her to take the job he was offering. He was successful, she got to make an informed choice and they all lived happily ever after.

If you are offered the job and want to take it, now is the time to iron out any remaining details. For example, you may not have discussed your pay in detail yet. If there's anything you want to check with your union, you might accept the post verbally but make it clear to the school that this is subject to taking some advice. Teachers are advised not to hand in their notice formally before they are happy with their new employer's contract. If you are unclear about the terms of your contract, seek clarification with the school and your union. The unions warn against accepting temporary and fixed-term contracts if a permanent post is available to you. If you have little choice, ask the school why the post is not permanent and discuss these reasons with your local associations if you are uneasy. Similarly, you're advised not to sign any contract with waiver clauses which undermine your employment rights.

If you do stay for what turns out to be a bitter end, a debriefing session is often offered to candidates. It is up to you whether you want to take it, but it can give you some useful pointers on how to present yourself and how you come over. Most interviewers are genuinely keen to see you succeed, even if they don't see it happening right now or at their school: you may well get some good career advice from an objective source.

MY FIRST JOB

After my physics degree, I did a PGCE, but I decided not to teach because I got a better offer – an acoustic design job which was right up my street. Having also just done teaching practice, I thought industry would be a lot less hard work. However, the PGCE was a really good start to my working life. I felt very confident about my capabilities after that year. I could run meetings, could explain and persuade – skills which were invaluable in dealing with clients and colleagues. I'd had to be organised and work hard. All in all I was much better equipped for work than after my degree and I stayed there four years.

But it all got rather dull. The projects and products I was working on were different but the methods were always the same, and the people. I only worked with six people on a regular basis. In teaching it's the opposite; there's no routine and every day is different. It's also one of the most purposeful jobs there is. In industry, I felt there was little point in what we were doing (and as the company went bust a year ago, that feeling was confirmed).

A job came up suddenly teaching science at a local school, when a teacher left at Christmas.

As an NQT it is difficult enough, but I was starting half-way through the year and teaching a lot of science outside my main subject. And I couldn't really remember what to do in a classroom – after four years in work, all I could remember about teacher training was having a good time in the pub in the afternoon. I was rescued by a colleague, who introduced me to the idea of setting the kids some work. I'd been trying to talk for an hour, and thought I was being experimental when I walked around the room a bit. When I stopped the constant whole class teaching, everyone was mightily relieved – me and the kids – to be getting on with things.

Now I've been teaching for a year, I've learnt to be flexible and adaptable in my thinking and systems. I couldn't possibly mark all the work I have to get my GCSE class through, so I got them to do presentation on the topics we'd covered, which was a much more effective and enjoyable way of assessing what they knew. A year ago, I'd never have thought of that. In general, the highs are now higher and there are fewer lows, but I need more stability and predictability in my working day before I take on any responsibility. Right now, I'm just interested in doing the job.

I do miss some aspects of industry, of course. Deadlines are utterly final in teaching, whereas in industry you could reorganise or postpone a project, and prioritise sensibly. We planned the work so we had time to get it right; now I always do things in a hurry and never get them perfect. I regret the lack of personal time during the day. I could walk out of the office and my lunch hour was mine to do with as I chose. Now, lunch simply doesn't happen. I've been surprised at how shy of computers my colleagues in the science department are, and how poor the software they have to work on. And the environment in teaching is so different. It would have been hilarious to bring one of our clients into a workplace like our staffroom – at a crucial meeting you'd all be sitting on grotty chairs at different heights. I miss the calm, the backup for my work, the real coffee ... and working in the evenings is a bind. I've no regrets though – I'm really enjoying teaching.

Choosing Your School

Rhodes Boyson, ex-head and Conservative MP, was heard to scoff at suggestions that class sizes made any differences to standards, on the basis that 'a good teacher can teach anywhere'. It's the same line as 'kids are kids wherever you go'.

But schools, like teachers, are individual. In teaching, to a much greater extent than in many other careers, where you work can make a huge difference to your experience and enjoyment. No one would suggest you got hitched because your partner fulfilled basic requirements – two arms, two legs and passable table manners – and staff have a relationship with their workplace which, if not quite a marriage, is more intense than in most jobs. It's therefore worth pausing before you start your job hunt to draw up a wish list. You may not end up in a position to be picky, but if you find yourself faced with much the same job descriptions from two separate schools, it may help your applications and interviews (see chapter 2) feel less like an episode of *Blind Date*.

Surely it should be easy? The notional 'good school' lies in a nice suburb and goes something like this: recently painted buildings, concerned parents, playing fields and a respectable place in the league tables. The children wear their uniforms nicely and there's not a lot of noise about. This is the estate-agent approach to choosing your school – think location, location, location. And there's no doubt about it; staff recruitment is seldom a problem for schools like this, even though 'catchment areas' are becoming more flexible. You're unlikely to have made a howling mistake if you end up working on the archetypal leafy avenue. In dating terms, this is one you could confidently take home to your parents.

But this is not the only kind of school worth working in. 'Good schools' are not necessarily equally good employers, although any school which handles its staff well is likely to reap the benefits elsewhere. Many of the most important factors in choosing a school will be practical, not PR-driven – working conditions, pay and what it will do for your experience and development. A school with low results or grotty buildings may frighten off some parents, but for you it could offer excellent teamwork amongst staff and pupils, an inspiring head who pushes training, and rising GCSE rates in your specialist area.

Next to consider will be the shape of your career. You may well want the balancing experience of different types of school at different stages, or a new challenge to wake yourself up. One inner-city maths teacher deliberately pursued a head of department job in a failing school, having spent the early years of his career and a stint as department deputy in a school not far from the estate agent's dream. 'I'd mention the name of the school I was thinking of applying to, and everyone would take a sharp intake of breath, so I knew it was right. Frankly, I wanted to see if I could make a difference, and I wasn't going to know that if I stayed in the school which had prepared me.'

After that, it's down to values and atmosphere much more than in many other jobs; many teachers deliberately choose their workplaces in line with their educational or social principles. Exposing yourself to a new workplace culture keeps you on your toes, but teachers generally want to feel part of an institution whose aims they respect. A good starting point is to play about with some vocabulary and see what rolls most easily off your professional tongue. Later, you can see whether your sources of information talk about a prospective school in the same language (and indulge in a little speculation as to what it means – just as you'd do with estate agents' particulars):

Caring? (Strong pastoral system, community spirit, under-achievement, holistic approach to children, possibly a school in a deprived area?)

Innovative? (Lively, lots of scope for taking on responsibility and managing new projects, staff like headless chickens?)

Committed to excellence? (High standards being achieved deliberately, by default, or being pursued? Challenging or pressurised, for staff and pupils?)

HOW TO FIND OUT WHETHER A SCHOOL IS 'GOOD'

Sources of information on a school will be varied. A recent Ofsted report will give very detailed information and judgements. League tables provide exam results out of context; the school prospectus should reveal what the school is aiming for and its culture, as well as factual information like administrations policy, curriculum choices and the school structure. Good sources of information are obviously parents and pupils of the school. There are also a growing number of consumer guides to schools in the state and independent sector which have reports on individual schools, and which you can look at in a library or bookshop. Examples are *The Equitable Schools Book* (Bloomsbury and the *Sunday Times*), *The Independent Guide to Independent Secondary Schools*, and others – worth a look, although, like any guide, their judgements can be partial.

For a more professional perspective and factual information on things like budgets and any planned school reorganisations, unions can give you information via local branches, as can the LEA. Word of mouth is invaluable, especially if you can get hold of a member of staff. If you are an NQT, your college tutor may be able to fill you in on schools in your local area. Your colleagues at your present school may be just the grapevine you need to tap into.

Lastly and most crucially, you'll visit the school if you get an interview and this is your best opportunity to get a feel for the place (see chapter 2). Schools are usually happy to let you visit before this if you ring to arrange it, and indeed encourage visits like these for senior appointments.

The NASUWT recommends that your judgements about a school should begin with the application process itself. Before getting to work on impressing them, pause to think what sort of impression they're making on you. Is the job description clear and coherent? Are you provided with plenty of information, like school development plans or department policies, and are contacts forthcoming if you need to know more? Are your initial encounters with the school friendly and productive? In general, do they seem to know what they're doing and what they want from you?

DECODING YOUR INFORMATION: QUESTIONS TO ASK

- *Do I agree with the aims of the school?* What values does the prospectus and information for staff emphasise? What kind of leadership does the head give? What are the school rules? What is its local reputation – caring, lively, academic, well-rounded? How is it perceived by staff, pupils and parents when compared with other local schools? What is the tone of the information?

- *Do I agree with its educational principles?* What are the priority areas in the school development plan, and why? What kind of syllabuses do they follow? How do they divide pupils into classes? What kind of work and teaching have I seen going on? What is the attitude towards exam success? How much extra-curricular activity is going on? What's in the department handbook?

- *How do staff and pupils get along?* What sort of interaction do you see in the corridor and through classroom windows? How are you viewed when you look into a full classroom? What's the atmosphere in the corridor between lessons? What are the children wearing, and what are the seating arrangements in the rooms? How do teachers talk about their classes? What is the state of the building, displayed work? Are the noises you hear buzzing and directed, or raucous?

- *Are teaching and learning resources good?* Look in book cupboards, on shelves for audio-visual equipment, in filing cabinets for prepared materials, in the library. Ask about department budgets, whether you'd have your own room and whether the department has a base, access to computers, support and technical staff, photocopying and time/money for trips.

- *How positive are morale and staff attitudes?* Does the department and the staffroom seem busy, sociable and cheerful? Is the seating ghettoised? Are there senior staff around at break? What notices are up and how much flow of information does there seem to be? What do staff say about the governors? What are staff wearing? What did the staff do to celebrate at Christmas?

- *How good is the school's staff development?* How are courses advertised? What further training would they expect to give you? Who has responsibility for what and how much are they paid? Will your job responsibilities change? What career expectations does the school seem to have of people in your post? What's your predecessor gone on to do? Where are they with appraisal? What have they spent their most recent INSET days on?

- *How much support for staff is there?* For example, bursars, science technicians, media resources officers, secretaries or librarians – who can ask for their help? Are there staff computers, quiet rooms for marking, basic catering facilities?

TYPES OF SCHOOL

Parents and pupils now have increasing diversity in the types of institution they can choose, so, added to schools' individual personalities, you might need to consider differences of funding and management of different types of school. How much of an impact would they have on your working life? What can you expect from the fact a school is, for example, voluntary-aided? Should you care?

The following section contains a high degree of generalisation – not ideal at the best of times, and definitely not a sensible deciding factor in choosing your workplace. To reiterate, schools have personalities all their own, and factors like the school leadership, the staff, the physical environment and the communities they serve are always *much* more important than constitutions. But for the sake of completeness, here are some of the main breeds. Note that some schools are hybrids – they may belong in a number of categories, like the girls' school which is a grant-maintained grammar, or a comprehensive, LEA-run, 11–16 city school! Note also that change is afoot in the very near future, as the constitutions of the different school types are reformed.

LEA SCHOOLS

Officially labelled 'county schools', very soon to become 'community schools' (but not necessarily of the type mentioned below), LEA-owned schools educate the vast majority of children. They can come in different shapes (comprehensive, grammar, special), age ranges and sizes, but are distinguished by the fact that they are non-denominational (not church schools) and are the legal responsibility of their governing bodies and the LEAs (who have representatives on governing bodies). All secondary schools now manage the vast majority of their money themselves, but the LEA holds 10 per cent of schools' budgets to finance the educational services it offers its schools. These services include the work of education welfare officers, special needs departments, advisers and inspectors, library and music services, teachers' centres, psychologists, school meals and cleaning. Although managed by the head on a day-to-day basis, the LEA school is also part of a network of schools and needs to respond in line with LEA strategic planning on, for example, the spread of school places in the borough. The LEA will have a say in the appointment of staff in its schools and run supply pools.

Working in an LEA school has all the potential advantages or disadvantages of any workplace with a parent company or head office. If the LEA is responsive to its schools and gives them access to helpful central services, allows them room to manoeuvre and provides them with leadership, exploits its capacity for economies of scale and concentrates expertise in its staff, then it will be popular. If it fails to do these things it will be a drag on schools' aims and actions. Although you wouldn't be able to change a bad situation, it's worth asking what the LEA is like, as an inspiring adviser or effective educational welfare officer could well be the icing on the cake for posts like head of department or head of year. For the development of an NQT, and indeed teachers in general, access to good LEA-wide training programmes could be a great bonus, getting you beyond the limits of your school and together with others in your situation and subject. In senior management roles it will have a significant impact on the nature of your experience, as more of your work will be linked to this outside agency (see chapter 4 for more).

Sandra Mohamed of the Local Schools Information Service, which gives information to schools undertaking ballots on grant-maintained status, says that working in an LEA system is becoming increasingly advantageous. After a period of cutbacks in advisory departments, there will be an upturn in the monitoring and advisory role of LEAs, with White Paper proposals making LEAs central to raising standards, 'and in the light of Ofsted, it is imperative for LEAs to support their schools by providing INSET, local fora and staff networks, which schools can call on freely'. Unattached schools, by contrast, 'have only Ofsted to see how they're doing'. She points to other possible bonuses for employment rights: 'LEAs might offer additional benefits – for example, on maternity or sick leave terms – beyond the statutory minimum. There is the chance of redeployment too if a school closes, and the right to be part of consultation exercises on LEA plans. And anecdotally, we do hear that some governors are reluctant to shortlist candidates who don't have a good grasp on the local scenario, which teachers get by being in an LEA school.' In addition, she points out that informal networks and staff contact between local schools can be an extremely useful resource for teachers.

COMPREHENSIVES

The comprehensive system, established in 1965, continues to be the main way in which education is organised in England and Wales and over 80 per cent of children are part of it. A comprehensive can be many things – a county school, grant-maintained, voluntary – but its one defining feature is that it offers education to local children of all abilities. Its admission policy usually gives priority to families within a certain radius of the school, and otherwise it takes all-comers. So for a teacher, the comprehensive offers breadth and variety.

The range of pupil ability requires a range of teaching methods. If the school operates mixed-ability teaching (although it may not do for much longer, depending on how explicit the present Government gets on this issue), there's the challenge of organising your lessons so that they can be effective and stimulating for both the brightest and the least able child. If the children are grouped according to their abilities in different subjects, you will have to switch your approach from lesson to lesson, depending on the class you're teaching. This keeps you fresh and there's the satisfaction of seeing pupils achieve according to their potential, whatever their 'level'. Attention to the individual and equal opportunities are especially important in such a school. And in the genuine local comprehensive there's the enjoyment of the social mix: you might be happiest in a melting pot. A diversity of experience, opinions, values and religions in your kids may also make lessons and discussions in your subject a lot more interesting.

It is important to check, nevertheless, how truly comprehensive a school is, as local circumstances will create a unique profile for the school. The other schools in the local area can have a significant effect. For example, if there's a selective or single-sex school down the road, the gender and ability mix won't be genuinely comprehensive, and it is worth asking what the actual profile of the intake is. Similarly, the nature of the local area – its housing, employment and social features – will be a big factor in the sort of attitudes you'll meet in the classroom.

Size and place can matter too. A large comprehensive will mean big departments and a breadth of subjects – this might be a good place to get your first middle-management experience (there will be more colleagues to liaise with and more students to consider, and possibly more delegation of responsibilities) and there will probably be more opportunities to teach newer or rarer courses at GCSE or A level, so your qualification in Classics or Media Studies may finally prove useful. At deputy and head level, salaries are also different according to the size of a school (of which there are five 'groups'). In a smaller school, you will get closer to more of the pupils; a teacher at a small mid-Wales comp says, 'Our kids aren't quite so streetwise and the relationship between the staff and pupils is very cosy, compared with the city schools I've worked in. Of course there are awkward kids, but because of the size of the school there are fewer of them and so they tend to fall into line because they are in the minority.' Rural schools are likely to have a particularly strong relationship with their community: the same teacher says, 'When teachers are also locals, there's a real sense of involvement. Parents, teachers, kids, everyone helps with productions, fund-raisers and so on.' Which is not to write off city schools, where children are frequently warm and sociable towards staff, nor to ignore the fact that smaller schools can get 'claustrophobic – the common room can get so political'.

CASE STUDY

Bob Salisbury has put his school – and himself – on the education map since he took over as head in 1989. The Garibaldi School in Mansfield was losing pupils, due to vandalism, poor results and a very negative local reputation. Today the school is visited as a model of improvement (by Prince Charles, amongst others), having been presented with a host of awards for its curricular work, personnel development and management. Bob Salisbury is in demand as a speaker on leadership and change, in both the education and commercial worlds.

He began his career as a teacher of Geography and English

in Nottinghamshire, but then went abroad for two years, working as a deep-sea fisherman, in the lumber industry and hotel catering. He returned to what he calls one of the most boring jobs of all time in a Midlands hosiery factory, before moving back into teaching as a deputy in English. He moved – still within Nottinghamshire and the comprehensive system – to a head of social studies and head of year job next, and then to a head of faculty (Humanities). A deputy job came next at the Alderman White School in Bramcote, as preparation for his headship, and he also spent ten years as Chief Examiner for NEAB Integrated Humanities. He has published numerous papers on teaching humanities, and school management.

I certainly did not plan a career path and, at least in the early days, the need to seek promotion seemed to coincide with the birth of each of our three sons!

What I love about my current job is the opportunity to make things happen, and having the freedom to challenge traditional ways of doing things. I know I would have found being a headteacher in the days before delegated budgets totally frustrating, and would perhaps by now have become cynical and resentful. The ever-changing circumstances in education now allow the use of innovation, enterprise and imagination, and that is certainly one of the things which gives me a professional buzz. The other is watching the growth in confidence and achievement amongst staff and students over the years and observing the realisation from the community that in a school like this, with its troubled history, things can be made to change.

The best decisions I ever made in my career were marrying my wife Rosemary and taking a Masters degree at Loughborough University. The first because my wife provides a constant high-level professional challenge to my thinking, and will bring me quickly back to earth when I become too pompous or arrogant. The second because additional study midway through a career does give a golden opportunity to consolidate a personal philosophy and to underpin this with current research.

The biggest mistake I made was not having the courage to take on conventional wisdom about the way schools should be run much earlier in my career. 'Playing safe, not making mistakes and maintaining the status quo' was the advice given by my line managers at the time, and on reflection that was false counsel.

My career advice would be: 'Don't put up with mediocrity for the sake of peace, and keep asking the question "Why?"'

GRANT-MAINTAINED SCHOOLS

Considering the number of mentions they've had – and continue to have – on the news and in politicians' speeches, you'd be forgiven for thinking that GM schools had become the norm in the education system; in February 1996 there were 645 GM secondaries, which represents a significant but hardly overwhelming 17 per cent of the total. However, their presence will be felt more or less according to the area you're looking to work in. What's been notable is the domino effect they have in an area – like buses, it's none at all or a stream of them all at once. The London Borough of Hillingdon contains only GM schools, whilst the LEA runs all the schools in neighbouring Harrow. In general they are more common in the south-east (Greater London, Essex and Kent), East Anglia and the north-west.

Like many of the school types mentioned in this section, GMs are facing restructuring and change to their constitutions in the very near future. Under the present regime, however, grant-maintained schools are distinctive because they have complete control over their budgets. The intention is to bring them more firmly back into contact with local structures, but it seems GM schools will still be funded directly by the government rather than via an LEA. GMs control the money which, for LEA schools, is held by the authority to provide central services, and are awarded special grants for staff development and governor training. They also get extra money to become GM, and bid for grants for building projects and equipment; it is inequalities of funding which have made GM unpopular in many quarters. This aside, the DfEE says, most GM schools get the same budget they would have received if they had stayed with the LEA – but if they can make savings when buying services the LEA used to buy for them (for example, school cleaning or caterers), then they can keep the money. Don't assume that GM schools have better resources; what the GM gains on room to manoeuvre might be balanced by an LEA's ability to bulk-buy and specialise.

The other key feature is that the governing body – with no LEA members – is responsible for the school, employs the staff and is legally accountable for its finances and educational provision, although organising and managing the school from day to day is the head's job. The fact that your contract is with the governing body and not an LEA does not affect your statutory rights at all – the GM school takes over where the LEA left off with pensions, redundancy and general employment rights. However, there are three areas to take care over. Your continuity of service will be lost if you move from an LEA to a GM school, and this may mean you are not eligible for certain benefits until you have served a fixed period of time (two years in relation to some maternity rights, for example). You may well lose additional benefits which have been negotiated with an LEA, such as improved sickness benefits; working in a GM school won't necessarily affect your non-statutory rights, but check arrangements out with your union as GM governors do not have to honour any preferential agreements you've been used to within an LEA (or indeed in your last GM school). Finally, since 1991, GM schools have been able to ask the Government for the right to set their own pay and conditions. Only a tiny number have their own scale, but check this.

A study by John Fitz, David Halpin and Sally Power found some common traits in the schools opting out in 1989–92. They were slightly more likely than LEA schools to be selective or ex-grammar, to have special admission criteria like church membership, to be single-sex, have a sixth form – in short, to be more traditional in ethos, with uniforms and codes of conduct to match. But many more schools have opted out since and for lots of different reasons. Despite the conservative image of GMs, there are comments like these to consider: 'My school went GM in order to remain comprehensive in an increasingly right-wing and pro-selective local authority area,' says a Wandsworth teacher.

It's much more common for opted-out schools to give pragmatic reasons for their status (e.g. to avoid reorganisation or closure by the LEA, to gain access to more money, or to do things their way) and many GM school teachers say it doesn't affect their daily life. However, it's important to discover why a school opted out, and what use it's now making of its independence. Once you know the circumstances, you will be better placed to know how GM status will affect your work in practice.

- *Internal relations.* Do the governors, head and staff see eye to eye, and how do they communicate? Was and is the staff split over opting out? How does the head wield his or her substantial power?

- *Your career.* Is staff development and INSET money well used? Is there a to-and-fro between staff in your school and local LEA schools? Are subject staff in touch with local associations or advisers? Are heads of department getting up to date information, for example, on National Curriculum developments? In senior positions, might lack of LEA contact in a professional capacity limit experience? Or will GM independence give you more freedom to lead and make decisions?

- *Networks.* What relations does the school have with the LEA now? What services is it still connected to in the area?

- *Money.* Why did the school want to control more of its money? Were there specific educational needs and aims which weren't being met? What has the extra cash been spent on? Are services better now?

- *Ethos.* Did the school opt out to protect or alter its character? Are there plans for it to become much bigger, or to change its admissions policy?

- *Employment.* Have any pay and conditions agreements been changed by the governors? Are benefit packages in line with local authority schools and national expectations?

Further general information on teaching in grant-maintained schools can be had from the DfEE leaflets 'Grant-Maintained Schools: A Brief Guide for School Staff' and 'Grant-Maintained Schools: Questions staff ask'.

INDEPENDENT SCHOOLS

Independent schools are privately run and pupils pay fees to attend them – as opposed to the 'maintained' schools which are state-run and maintained by public taxes. Their image is very fixed – high standards, good discipline, a traditional ethos and a privileged intake – but in practice, private schools are as varied as those in the state system, aiming themselves at a particular niche in the market. It is certainly true that some independents achieve very high academic standards, and for teachers considering this sector, small class sizes and well-equipped classrooms will be an attraction. ISIS, the information service for the private system, cites these two factors and adds other benefits: freedom to concentrate on teaching rather than administration and discipline, an unusual degree of parental support, a strong emphasis on extra-curricular activities, high take-up at A level, and a much more diverse social mix than is commonly thought (due to the now doomed Assisted Places Scheme). Most independents teach the National Curriculum, although legally they need not; they might not take part in all national tests.

As Head of Theatre Studies at a St Albans independent, Noel Cassidy says that

> physical conditions are better in the independents I visit as a moderator, compared with most state schools. Freedom is granted by more money. If I want to teach a text at A level, I can go ahead and order it, rather than being dictated to by the stock cupboard. There is also less bureaucracy. For example, we don't have to sit the SATs, and the organisation of extra-curricular visits is simpler, which is an important factor in my subject area. I hear tales of endless form-filling from drama specialists in state schools, whereas I can be so much more responsive. If someone offers me twelve cheap tickets for a production that week, I can say yes, get in the minibus with the kids and go. Beyond

that, the differences between the two sectors can be exaggerated. I've been frequently amazed by the standards of some state schools' coursework.

Terms and conditions can be more generous, given that the private sector is free to pay above the national scale. Schools which are members of professional associations pay at least national rates, often adding a percentage to the state-system pay scale, and sometimes operating generous salary scales unique to the school. Most teachers in independents are still members of the national pension scheme. In return, the teaching day is frequently longer in the independent sector, but there can be a higher proportion of non-contact time (that is, time free to mark and prepare). Hours vary a great deal, given the major contribution of staff to clubs, outdoor pursuits and other activities beyond the school day, and this is even more true in boarding schools, where teachers' pastoral work extends way beyond their teaching day. Holidays are a little longer than in the state system, significantly so in the boarding schools. Part-time work can be a great deal easier to come by in private schools, too.

There is mobility between independent and maintained schools, albeit limited. The differences between state and independent sector are very much to do with perception, although independent-sector teachers who train on the job and have no qualifications won't find openings in the state system. State-school governors sometimes assume that independent-sector teachers are limited in their teaching repertoire, which is not necessarily fair given that not all private schools are fiercely academic and selective. Whereas independent governors can be snobbish. There is a perceived lack of discipline and academic rigour in the maintained sector, and applicants from state schools have been asked interview questions like 'What are your research interests?' ISIS says teachers should not fear getting sidelined in the independent sector: 'Most schools are in tune with developments ... and have introduced many positive contributions familiar in the maintained sector.' A good look at teaching and assessment practices, school initiatives and staff development will tell you whether you will keep in touch with what is happening nationally. Look also for membership of professional associations and accreditation by the Independent Schools Joint Council, which inspects and reviews the work of private schools.

ISIS also argues that 'with the ending of the formal probation period for newly qualified teachers, there is no professional disadvantage to teachers starting their careers in independent schools' and that induction for NQTs is well thought out in many schools. (They will, however, need to react to the White Paper proposal to re-introduce a formal induction year.) The Headmasters Conference (HMC) says that training on the job can be arranged, whereby a student teacher can follow an Open University PGCE course whilst working in one of their schools, or aim for a qualification from the Centre for British Teachers. The vast majority of teachers in schools belonging to the associations have qualifications to teach, but this is the one area of the profession where you can be employed straight from university. Noel Cassidy did just this, during a period of unemployment whilst running a theatre company. Having stayed in the profession ever since, he does not feel the lack of formal training: 'Most people who've done a PGCE say that teaching practice was the really valuable part of it, and I was in full-time practice.'

Information on teaching in independent schools in general is available from ISIS, who can also provide lists of schools in your area. More detailed information about individual schools comes from the relevant professional body (Girls' School Association, Headmasters' and Headmistresses' Conference, Independent Schools Association and Society for Headmasters and Headmistresses of Independent Schools). Schools advertise via the *TES* in a discrete section – there are no central bodies recruiting for the independent sector. Independents do use specialist recruitment agencies (T. Gabbitas, QED, START); supply teachers or young people looking for a year-off job in a school environment (here or abroad) can also contact the School Appointment Service. Lastly, the Professional Association of Teachers publishes a booklet, written by its solicitor, David Brierley, called 'Independent Schools', covering employment rights, contract, pay, pensions and many other areas of pay and conditions, and costing £3.40 (free to PAT members).

VOLUNTARY SCHOOLS

Until the changes due in autumn 1999, the 'voluntary' sector includes three types of school – voluntary-aided, voluntary-controlled, and special agreement schools – so named because they were established by a voluntary organisation. This founder is usually a religious body, which is why they are more popularly thought of as 'church schools'.

The differences between the three types of 'church school' lie in how they are financed and managed. Aided schools have less connection with the LEA, although the LEA pays for staff, internal repairs and general costs; the voluntary body controls the governing body, pupil admissions and staff appointments, and pays for the exterior of the school. In controlled schools, the influence of the LEA is greater: the LEA nominates two-thirds of the governors, finances everything and employs the staff. Special agreement schools are a mixture of the two, but the most relevant point for teachers is that, as in controlled schools, the LEA and not the governing body is the employer. As with any type of school where founders or governors have special powers, it is worth asking how the relationship with the teaching staff works. (See the list of questions for GM schools.) Voluntary schools can also be wealthy, due to parental contributions, although again this money may not affect teachers directly.

Church schools have an enviable reputation with the general public, and they do appear to get good results and foster a good atmosphere for pupils and staff. Why is this? One church school teacher says firmly that the intake – the majority from church-going, middle-class, concerned backgrounds – is the key. She adds, 'But there is also the extra focus which the children have, even if their faith isn't particularly strong. They feel they are here to learn to be more compassionate, and there is the sense in the school that we are a community and a family.' A newly appointed head of department in a Catholic school noted, 'I'm not religious myself and was a little apprehensive about teaching in a church school. But I've been very pleased by the way the values of the school have affected my experience – here are thirteen year olds who were asked to reflect every morning at prayers, and you can see that thoughtfulness coming out in their work and attitudes.' The family feeling can also extend to the staff: 'There is a feeling of well-being and of looking out for one another which I'm not sure I've seen in other schools. When my stepfather died, the head (a vicar) wrote me a moving letter, and the deputies routinely put up notes about events in people's lives which have called them away, so that they are supported when they return.'

Lack of religious belief is not a bar to being employed by a church school – adverts usually ask for candidates who will be in sympathy with the school's religious values. (In management, things are different – one teacher says his swift journey up the career ladder in a C of E school came to an abrupt halt at senior teacher level because he was not a practising Christian: 'It makes sense – I couldn't give the kind of leadership they needed.') The schools' status does not affect what children are taught – religious schools follow the National Curriculum like everyone else, with RE as an added core subject for all pupils; in addition, they can offer teaching of their own religion, whereas other schools must offer non-denominational RE to their pupils. Those with a firm religious faith can, however, express this in extra-curricular contexts – religious study groups, fellowships, visits and camps.

SINGLE-SEX SCHOOLS

Single-sex schools were generally established in times when young men and women were not encouraged to rub shoulders (or anything else), or by charitable foundations whose remit embraced girls or boys but not both, or by founders with a belief in the benefits or propriety of single-sex education. With this background, they are often traditional places – selective, academic, formal – and in general, says one school inspector, 'The single-sex schools I visit are less relaxed than co-eds.' Like church schools, their pupils (girls in particular) often excel in examination terms. Also like church schools, they can occasionally be more idiosyncratic in character than your ordinary sixties-built comp – one teacher on interview remembers being appraised not only by the head but also by the large and hairy dog underneath her desk. Another young drama teacher was rapped across the proverbial knuckles by his gowned principal for 'over-familiar behaviour' when he was seen eating an apple in the presence of a student at break-time.

But just as often, they can be innovative and ambitious institutions which work wonders with young people's confidence and wider interests in an environment free, they argue, from the expectations and pressures of the opposite sex. Some teachers are dedicated to the equal opportunities (not only for their charges but for themselves) which they see flourishing in single-sex institutions, and wouldn't work anywhere else. At the same time, you can encounter gender issues at their most sensitive: 'We had to remember that many of our girls came from cultural backgrounds which put limits on their academic ambitions. We could get caught in the cross-fire between some parents – who'd chosen our school to protect their girls – and "rebellious" daughters whose interests we tried to represent. Or we'd get the attitude, "I'm getting married soon, so what's the point of even sitting my GCSEs?"' says a teacher working in the London Borough of Tower Hamlets.

There are probably no advantages or disadvantages about single-sex schools that aren't covered by the standard – and therefore unreliable – generalisations made about male and female working environments:

Boys' schools are more aggressive. But once they're on your side, they are very loyal. It helped that I was like them – a local girl, supported the same football team, Catholic – and that I wasn't very young nor very pretty. And you have to be very tough, right from the start.

Single-sex teaching is not as rewarding as mixed, unless the school is addressing the issues of single-sex education.

I loved the confidence of the girls, in their academic and extra-curricular activities. It was working with a staff made up almost entirely of women that I didn't enjoy as much!

SPECIFIC AGE-RANGE SCHOOLS

The pros and cons of schools which are not comprehensive are fairly obvious – they give a more intense experience of some kinds of teaching, and less of others. It is of course perfectly possible to get a more partial experience in a mixed school if you teach exclusively upper-school subjects like business studies or economics or media studies; you may teach subjects which attract the less or more able at Key Stage 4; you may work in an old-fashioned set-up where individual teachers are tacitly but routinely given certain types of classes because 'they're good with naughty kids' or are considered 'A level teachers'. Common sense will however tell you the experience you will – and won't – get in schools which don't cater for the full range of pupils. If the school seems to provide a good experience, then missing out on this range may not matter for a period in your career, and especially not if you make the most of the focus of attention on certain phases of education, to give depth to your practice.

A PGCE allows you to work in all phases of secondary education, which covers institutions catering for young people between the ages of eleven and eighteen. Most comprehensives admit the full age range, but the British system also includes 11–16 schools, upper schools and sixth-form colleges. (There are also 8–13 middle schools, but these are few and far between in the state system).

Upper schools take pupils aged thirteen or fourteen upwards and are going to be very focused on GCSE work and usually have a strong post-sixteen emphasis too, so can be good in providing opportunities for vocational teaching (GNVQs) and using your more arcane specialities at A level – but you'll miss full experience of the Key Stage 3 curriculum. The 11–16 schools will be great at focusing the attention on progression from KS3 to KS4, but won't provide the A level teaching valued by most secondary teachers as the means of keeping in touch with their subject. One assistant of head of history says, 'I'm a deputy now but I'm probably going to need to make a sideways move to get the A level experience for head of department jobs.' (Whilst some LEAs operate extremely successful 11–16 school systems, there has been debate whether schools without sixth forms 'work' as social and educational institutions, because of the lack of role models for younger pupils and intellectual satisfaction for staff.)

Working in post-sixteen education involves more differences than a particular curriculum emphasis. Hilary Compton did a PGCE, and her teaching practice was at an 11–16 school, but now works in a sixth-form college in Surrey.

When I began, we were subject to school regulations, but that's changed. Our structure was much like a school, with assemblies, form time and so on. Now we're on a lecturers' pay scale, terms and conditions. Lecturers' pay has fallen – as well as being an experienced teacher, I'm a co-ordinator for a course involving eighty students, eight weeks of work experience and a lot of test administration, and I'm on £21,000 pro rata. Our holidays have been cut by two weeks, with another ten days now discretionary. And promotion is scarce – only 10 per cent of lecturing posts are promoted, and very little time is given to discharge responsibilities. When I was Head of Biology, I managed a ten-strong department, twenty A level groups, and had one hour free in the week to deal with all related departmental work!

Her part-time timetable includes A level Biology and GNVQ in Health and Social Care, for which she is the course co-ordinator, and she also teaches an evening class at the college. She got into Further Education without having deliberately pursued this kind of teaching, although she does say she had misgivings about the full range in secondaries.

I'd done a Ph.D. and was really enthusiastic about biology, and was looking forward to sharing this with the kids. I really enjoyed the lower-school teaching but the middle years of Year 9 and 10 had been difficult. It was demoralising to find that lots of them weren't interested in the subject; I got on with them fine but only after I'd adjusted to the idea that we weren't going to cover much biology.

Her move to FE, teaching only A level, put this right, but she wanted to extend her range and so moved colleges to get experience of vocational post-sixteen teaching as it was beginning to be introduced.

I taught BTEC and now GNVQ. Vocational courses are hard work. There need to be lots of meetings between the numerous tutors teaching different parts of the course, as opposed to the two who usually team-teach an A level course. Assignment marking is a nightmare too, as you're assessing coursework on so many different criteria – I mark twenty A level essays in the time it takes me to get through one GNVQ assignment. However, I really like teaching the courses (and there's word that the Government are going to overhaul the assessment). It's so pleasing to see these students do well on the courses, when they wouldn't on an A level course – not because it's easier but because it's different. Their presentations are brilliant – much better than beginning teachers! I also have to do research for the courses which are outside my normal area – for example, I've been looking at the new structures in the NHS. Between the A level and GNVQ, I do get stretched.

In the future she would like to move into the college management, or perhaps back into schools:

I know I would have a lot of convincing to do at an interview, given that I've only done a teaching practice with eleven to sixteen year olds and the occasional lessons with GCSE students when they come to visit the college. When I interviewed for my present college, I had no experience of BTEC so I made sure I read a lot about it, the syllabuses and so on. I'd have to do the same for the pre-sixteen curriculum if I went for a school interview. But I do have a lot to offer schools. Schools don't have a lot of experience of vocational courses. And I do have a good range of teaching skills – our A level styles are varied, and the GNVQ teaching style is very flexible, with lots of negotiation, group and individual work and project work.

SELECTIVE SCHOOLS

The only type of school which seems specially avoided by some on ideological grounds is the selective school. Principles seem to be mentioned more where grammars are involved, and self-interest in relation to secondary moderns. Many state-school teachers are opposed to selection; others simply want to stay in touch with the range of ability. As usual there are divergent opinions on whether there are benefits to working in a selective setting – it's either a paradise or pressure cooker:

I began teaching in an independent grammar, which was not only selective but highly so. It was not until I moved on from there that I realised that teaching was a job, and that you had to work; 'teaching' at the grammar had in fact meant chairing discussions, and occasionally intervening to stop one pupil becoming dominant. And just as lessons were more like seminars, the staff saw themselves more as academics. Interviewees would do well to think about their own subject interests and qualifications.

versus

I spend all my time keeping up with them. They eat through the work so fast, and there's so much marking.

There's no reason to assume that teachers who deal with only very able or less able pupils are limited in the range of techniques they employ, both to teach and to motivate. Applicants moving to or from a selective school should analyse exactly what range of teaching styles they have, and mention this in their applications.

COMMUNITY SCHOOLS

Whilst the term 'community school' may come to mean LEA schools as the 1997 White Paper is implemented, the original community schools are part of an interesting movement in education. Providing education for all in the local area, community schools exist in clusters across the country, in urban and rural locations. They are particularly common in areas like Oxfordshire, Cambridgeshire, Kent and Scotland, although different authorities have developed the idea in their own way. Phil Street, director of the Community Education Development Centre which promotes community education, says that community schools 'operate without the traditional boundaries of secondary schools. Community schools aren't just dual-use buildings; they are schools which see themselves as providing learning opportunities for the wider community.' Some community schools do concentrate only on putting their resources to good use out of school hours, particularly to provide a venue for sport and night classes, and possibly using their staff to offer courses to wider clientele than their eleven to eighteen year olds. But in the kind of community schools that Phil Street means, the links between school and community are stronger, and the experience for teachers is more distinct.

Laurence Leader is director of Community Education at Heathfield Community School in Taunton, a deputy-level post funded by Somerset LEA, which has a network of twenty-four community schools. He stresses that every community school is different, partly because they reflect the individual communities in which they are located and partly because they are developed by different staffs. Teachers can therefore expect unique experiences, but in general, community schools are 'not for the traditional teacher who works in the classroom between 9 a.m. and 3.30 p.m. They are for teachers who enjoy making a difference, and who teach the student rather than their subject; they recognise they are teaching people, and enjoy seeing the benefits their work can bring to the whole community.' A dance evening performed by special-needs adults was a recent project in the school, organised by a teacher who was freed up to work part-time in the school and part-time with the adults. She enlisted the help of eleven and twelve year old students, and social services and a local dance agency were also involved. The school is the agent for two lottery applications, which it hopes will result in funding for sports and arts projects in the community.

Teachers here must enjoy creating something new, and innovations can come from the simplest things. A woman rang the school and said she'd like to attend a course we were running but couldn't get a babysitter, and could we help? We couldn't recommend a particular one of our fifteen year olds, so what staff did instead was set up a baby-sitting training course for students, run by the Red Cross. All we're doing is matchmaking – matching needs with resources.

SPECIAL SCHOOLS

There are a huge range of schools which cater for children who have special educational needs. They can vary in management – some are LEA-run, some independent, some GM, and some are non-profit-making but run by charities – and in the age groups they admit (although the trend is moving away from schools catering for very wide age ranges). They fall into a number of need categories, the main ones being:

> Moderate learning difficulties
> Severer learning difficulties
> Profound and multiple learning difficulties
> Emotional and behavioural difficulties
> Dyslexia
> Speech, hearing or visual impairment
> Autism
> Cerebral Palsy

Teachers who want to work in special education are often encouraged to work in mainstream education first, so that they can be better informed about the relative needs and experience of children in special schools. Also, most teachers working in special schools have gained their SEN experience, INSET and training in a mainstream setting – see chapter 5 for details. You don't need specific qualifications to work in a special school, unless you are working with hearing or visually impaired pupils. In this case, you need to become specifically qualified within three years of taking up your post.

Working in special education can be intensely rewarding, and the career structure in special schools is clearer than for mainstream support teachers. You need to have the kind of qualities expected in any teacher – but obviously great patience and excellent communication skills, as well as an informed understanding of your pupils' particular needs, is required. One head of support services says that flexibility is crucial. A child with special needs in one area is very likely to have related needs – so you've got to be able to recognise and support them across all their difficulties.

SPECIALIST SCHOOLS: TECHNOLOGY COLLEGES, LANGUAGE, ART AND SPORT COLLEGES, AND CTCS

From 1993, the last Government began to offer schools the opportunity of becoming providers of a specialist education, with a strong vocational emphasis. The first initiative was directed at science and technology; the technology schools' mission was 'to aim to provide the excellent practical technological, scientific, mathematical and communication skills needed by the manufacturing and service industries of our country'. Later, the specialist initiative was extended to the areas of modern languages, and bids opened for schools wanting to be centres of excellence for the arts and sports. By June 1997, there were 180 technology colleges, 42 language colleges, 6 sport schools and 3 arts schools, with 124 schools affiliated to the Technology Colleges Trust. In addition, there remain 15 City Technology Colleges, the mainly independent industry-sponsored schools on which the maintained specialist schools concept is based. In the future they are likely to become more connected to their local area through the introduction of LEA governors.

The specialist school initiative looks set to continue. The intention is to take pupils further than normal in these subject areas. The National Curriculum continues to be taught so that pupils receive a broad and balanced education, but in addition they are exposed to improved teaching, extra-curricular activities and facilities in the specialist area. This might mean a greater emphasis on these subjects than is normal in the timetable, more input from professionals involved in the specialism, and strengthened links between the school and industry. (The financing of the schools is in part by sponsors from the specialist area.) So, in an arts college, pupils might be expected to gain at least two good GCSEs in arts subjects and work with practising performers or artists. In a technology school's sixth form, the aim would be to increase the numbers of pupils sitting A levels or vocational courses in science or mathematics subjects, and to provide careers guidance which encouraged pupils to pursue vocational and academic courses in these areas, or to become employed in technology-related fields.

For staff who are involved in the teaching of the specialism, these schools clearly offer interesting experiences. One head of modern languages enthused that her job is never dull since the school became a language college, and mentions the spin-offs it has presented ('I've got onto the "Speaking at languages conferences" bandwagon rather by mistake. This might lead to other avenues which would be an alternative promotion within the teaching hierarchy.') INSET for the key subject specialists has to be a major feature in specialist schools' plans: foreign exchanges, work shadowing or industry placements might be available. For a specialism teacher, there would obviously be a buzz in working in an institution dedicated to your field, and where all pupils are enthusiastic about and often talented in your subject (given that the schools are allowed to introduce some element of selection based on pupils' aptitude in the specialist areas). There might be promotion possibilities which are not to be found in a normal secondary – the head of music in an arts college would find him or herself centre stage, probably higher up in the school hierarchy and exposed to new managerial opportunities.

For teachers of subjects other than the specialism, there may be a niggling sense of being a second-class citizen. Doubts are easily answered by gauging the morale of those departments not in the limelight, their involvement in the work of the college, and looking at the practical pointers to 'equal opps' for all staff members (e.g. how points are distributed amongst staff and so on). Improved provision of the specialism can have useful perks for all curriculum areas: increased access to technology such as satellites, Internet, audio and video equipment, multilingual news services, as well as plain old WPs, can work wonders in many subjects.

As far as prospects and conditions go, such a school may have something to offer. Cross-curricular links between staff may be more common in a school with a strong focus, and this might be valuable experience for your CV if you feel you've only really managed projects within your own subject area. Extending curriculum time in the specialism areas will affect the timetable, and teachers in some specialist schools end up working a slightly less traditional school day. TOIL (time off in lieu) may be on offer – in return for one late teaching day, you could be freed up for an afternoon of sport, study, a hobby, or some tutoring.

Chalk Another One Up: Career Progression

'Go for posts because you'll enjoy them, and be good at them – not because of the money or just because you can.'

Head of Science, eighteen years in teaching

PROMOTION

There are many paths towards career progression, and many teachers would rather not embark on the one which leads out of the classroom. Even those who are ambitious for senior managerial roles say they regret the 'choice' between promotion and contact with children, as their timetable loses more and more teaching periods. However, promotion up the management ladder is still the most visible measure of success in teaching, and 60 per cent of secondary teachers were in posts of responsibility on 1997 estimates (many more than in the primary sector).

This is also where teaching becomes the handling of big as well as little people, as those in posts of responsibility take on the job of motivating, managing, developing, informing, assessing and monitoring adult colleagues. One Head of Science says, 'What I most enjoy about my current job is the opportunity to introduce new ideas and insights into my subject – or life in general! – with pupils *and* staff.' As you would expect from teachers, managers (and particularly middle managers) say the people-orientated part is the attraction of moving up, as well as the greater involvement with planning pupils' and subjects' development. The increase in 'paperwork' is not so popular, nor is there always a proper time allocation – the work of departmental and pastoral heads accompanies a busy teaching timetable, whilst senior management work long hours outside the school day. The School Teachers' Review Body found recently that an increasing number of teachers are questioning the point of promotion, as a result.

But promotion gives the power to make things happen, get involved and follow through interests, as the following comments show:

'Promotion plays an important part in my plans because I am a passionate believer in education, and want to be in a position to influence change and inspire others.'
Deputy head in charge of KS4, fifteen years in teaching

'I most enjoy being able to have an impact on the department as a whole, and improving teachers' and students' experience of lessons.'
Head of Geography, three years in teaching

'Don't wait for jobs to be given or created. Promotion has always come after I have been performing particular roles.'
Head of English, sixteen years in teaching

POINTS

'Career success means I'm now in a very fortunate financial position,' says a senior teacher with thirteen years' experience, underlining the fact that promotion is also the only route to more money. Experience and annual pay rises can only take you so far (to point 9), and if teachers take on more responsibility, they are rewarded with points which move them up the Common Pay Spine. The maximum responsibility points teachers can add is five (at senior teacher level). Deputy or head teachers are paid on completely different salary spines, which are also affected by the size of their school. (See Appendix B for these senior salary ranges.)

There are different kinds of responsibility points available. The most common are the permanent allowances which accompany certain jobs – if you move from the job, you obviously lose the points. In secondary schools, the most commonly awarded allowance is for two points, compared with one in primary schools. Only an estimated 4 per cent are temporary awards, when a job is finite and project-like – for example, developing and implementing a policy on a new national initiative. In theory, teachers can also be awarded excellence points for their work in the classroom; in practice, very few heads make these awards, as discussed in Chapter 1. Special-needs teachers working in special schools are also awarded one or two points for their work and their qualifications.

PROSPECTS

Partly because of earlier retirement (especially by heads) and partly because of schools' poverty, people are reaching quite senior managerial positions younger (although a 1995 survey of headteacher vacancies notes that 'worryingly, a historically low proportion of the teaching force is below the age of thirty'). Barry Gandee of the NASUWT says, 'My advice is to go for promotion as soon as you feel you can – schools are looking for maximum experience within the minimum years of teaching, as this is cheaper for them.'

This is good news for those who want to rise fast. There are, however, a few drawbacks to youthful promotions, and not only for the teacher considered 'too old' or 'too expensive'. There may not be the leisure to take the advice of this deputy head: 'Perfect your classroom practice before seeking further promotion.' A Head of Science likewise suggests: 'After a couple of years in teaching, pause, do something like an MA, before you get weighed down with too many responsibilities.' Another danger is of course that there's nowhere to go after the first flurry of promotion. An adviser says, 'My husband got his first job at twenty-four and by twenty-nine he was a head of department. It's not at all unusual to become a head of department by the time you're thirty. But what career progression is left to such people? A deputy head's role is completely different, and there's limited scope elsewhere for those who want to teach and be involved in curriculum development. It should be harder to be a head of faculty. You shouldn't be able to get there by the time you're thirty, and you should be there because you're a better and more experienced teacher than anyone else in your department.'

Age aside, gender is an issue in promotion patterns. The NUT's latest figures suggest that women are under-represented in the upper echelons of schools. Their posts are less likely to be promoted ones, and whilst women make up 50 per cent of the teaching force in secondary schools, 80 per cent of headteachers are men. This may be a changing picture of course; the 1996 STRB workload survey found that, on average, female deputies are younger than their male counterparts, and so may be waiting in the system. A head of modern languages at senior teacher level expresses the usual dilemma for people with outside commitments:

> It's difficult. I am still ambitious on one level, although I've never been 100 per cent convinced that I want to go further up the teaching hierarchy. It's now even more problematic since I became a mother at the age of forty. Despite all my feminist principles, I can't convince myself that my son would not lose out if I had to work the sort of hours at school a head does, and I really can't see the point of being a deputy if you're not going to be a head – I've got more autonomy and power in my current position. I need to try and keep a balance between family and career, and there is a conflict.

Neither is there much headway with other under-representation endemic in society, although for some groups, the issue is not really about the speed of promotion but under-representation in the profession as a whole (see chapter 2). Black teachers are concentrated in lower grades and in areas concerned with the needs of ethnic minority pupils and in shortage subjects. Similarly, only one in 125 women teachers is a secondary head compared with one in thirty male teachers. If certain groups are under-represented in positions of authority, then there is obviously a tremendous waste of potential and valuable talent. It is important also that pupils see women, black people and people with disabilities in positions of responsibility.

If progress on equal opportunities is hardly speedy, one NQT recently transferred from industry observes: 'Teaching is at least a democratic framework to work in . . . equal opportunities are seen as important, probably because they are so crucial in dealing with the kids. In industry, favouritism can be much more obvious, and the networks much more exclusive.' The use of person specifications in the shortlisting process and equal-opportunity interviewing are widespread, and schools and LEAs should have clear equal-opportunities policies which staff can consult and refer to, to back their cases. Equal-opportunities statements on adverts ('Applications are welcome from all sections of the community regardless of sex, ethnic origin, disability or sexuality') are also something to look out for.

Movement between schools is important for career success. It is the norm for people to move schools to get promoted, partly because their paths may be blocked where they are, but mainly because breadth of experience is valued, and of course healthy. A typical move might come three to six years into your career, to a first middle-management job – a deputy job, for example. Later moves might be made by year heads moving to head of school jobs, heads of department going sideways to larger departments, or deputies to their own departments. Deputies and heads are often – if not usually – external appointments. Moving can make the new job easier too – given the consensus-seeking style of school management, it can be much easier to arrive a fully-fledged middle-manager than to subtly change your position with your colleagues. One acting deputy said: 'I've been grateful for the experience of being an acting deputy, but I'd rather get a confirmed position elsewhere. I've found it difficult to tackle one of my colleagues on the fact that she's not following the department's policy; I'm so used to working shoulder to shoulder with her.' And moving from the scene of your first job is usually recommended; most NQTs do only two or three years in their first job, or a little more if they've been given responsibility worth staying for.

This migration between schools keeps staffrooms fresh, as well as extending personal CVs. The only drawback is that perfectly good internal candidates are sometimes overlooked: 'A friend works in publishing, and she says that when they look for someone to undertake a particular project, they always look at their own staff first to see who could do it. But in teaching I feel that external appointments are sometimes made on principle – getting in "new blood" without a thought for the capabilities, development and morale of internal candidates.'

However, you probably won't have to move to get a one-point or occasionally even a two-point responsibility. They are much more likely to go to internal 'candidates', may not be subject to an interview in the usual sense, and are often given for very specific duties, or to reward work already going on. A recurrent piece of advice from those on the career ladder is to volunteer and get involved; opportunities will follow.

If you feel you aren't getting a fair deal where promotion is concerned, for any reason, you could speak to your line manager, head, or school or local union rep, depending on the situation. Your staff development teacher – probably a senior teacher or deputy head – is also worth talking to, to discuss INSET or new duties, which might break the rut you've found yourself in. One deputy head in charge of staff development says, encouragingly, 'Seek help from within your organisation – people will help you if you know what you want.'

CASE STUDY

Margaret Maden has experience of being at the top of many education ladders. Her first post was as an assistant teacher of Geography at Stockwell Manor Comprehensive in London. She lectured at the Sidney Webb College of Education, before moving to a deputy headship at Bicester Comprehensive, and four years later she became Head of Islington Green Comprehensive. She next took on directorship of Islington 6th Form Centre, which led to tertiary advising for the old Inner London Education Authority. She was deputy education officer at Warwickshire before her appointment to chief education officer in the same authority. She left this post in 1995 and is now a part-time Professor of Education at Keele University.

The best thing about working in education is its importance, and the difference it makes to individuals, as well as to the wider society. I feel strongly that our own education and continued learning matter a great deal if we work in education. Unless this is understood and valued, then I don't see how we can be respected by learners or effective as managers.

The best decisions I've ever made are those which have enabled me to move between teaching, headship, local government and now 'academe'. Similarly, to have moved between inner London and the 'provinces' has enlarged my understanding and knowledge about differences and similarities between the city and the shires.

I have also learnt a lot about the larger UK education system by being a member of the National Commission on Education, established by Sir Claus Moser in 1991, and by being involved in the work of the Organisation for Economic Co-operation and Development in Paris. Learning about other countries helps you to understand your own better.

I can't think of any major regrets or mistakes in my career. Perhaps I've suppressed them in the darker recesses of my mind! I've never really planned my career, but, instead, have gone for slightly risky openings when these have arisen. Not being responsible for dependants or spouse must have helped in this.

POSITIONS

Teaching is definitely a hierarchical profession, although relations between staff and their line managers are usually quite democratic – autocratic rank-pulling isn't seen as effective. (Even heads see themselves as 'delegative' and 'favouring consensus' in their management style, according to a 1996 study by Jirasinghe and Lyons.) However, one attractive aspect of the profession is that a member of staff's place in the hierarchy can be different according to which plane you look along. Teachers in posts of responsibility will, as we saw in chapter 3, still have additional team roles and professional relationships 'below and sideways' from their place on the ladder. The head may also be a member of the technology department, the head of Year 8 might also be head of girls' PE, and a deputy head of history might also assist the exam secretary.

What exactly posts involve, their salaries and how they are combined will differ from school to school, even if they come under the same title of, for example, 'deputy'. The content of jobs may be linked to individuals' experience, 'how we've always done it' or policy innovations, but good employment practice should ensure reasonable parity across and within schools. There will also be quirks according to the specialist nature of a school – the head of IT in a technology school will have a higher profile than usual; and responsibility for community relations, which might form only part of a deputy's job in most schools, would fill a senior job in a community college. The points and pay attached to different jobs may also vary a little according to 'local circumstances' so a deputy in a Group 5 school (see chapter 3) will be paid more than in a Group 4, as might the head of learning support in a school where 70 per cent of the pupils came from homes where English was a second language.

However, there is a pattern. Until you get to senior management level, there are distinct pastoral and curriculum jobs. It's generally considered good to mix and match jobs from both areas, although teachers often have a preference. Here are the positions often found in large maintained secondaries, grouped according to their place on the ladder and in the pastoral/curriculum 'camps'.

SENIOR MANAGEMENT

HEADTEACHER

This is the job at the top of the school management tree – which only about 2 per cent of secondary teachers reach. Leadership – rather than management – is the current buzzword where heads are concerned and it's often said that the most fundamental element in a school's success is the quality of the head. With the introduction of delegated school budgets, financial management was added to the head's educational role – some large comprehensives are the biggest businesses in their local area, with substantial budgets – and for a while there was concern that this business role and the rate of change was 'affecting our ability to monitor the effectiveness of the curriculum and fulfil the role of a head teacher effectively' (NAHT Survey of Headteachers 1992). There seems to have been a determined effort to shake off this paperbound image and promote the elements of headship which require vision and pedagogic leadership. The Teacher Training Agency consultation group, which put together a national professional qualification for headship (NPQH), says the core purpose of a headship is 'To provide professional leadership for a school which secures its success and improvement, ensuring high quality education for all its pupils and improved standards of learning and achievement', a purpose firmly focused on the head's educational role.

Nevertheless, in pursuit of this educational success and improvement, the modern headteacher has a huge remit and a high profile in most areas. He or she has overall responsibility for strategic planning and monitoring of the school's objectives, finances and human resources; managing, developing and motivating staff and pupils; ensuring that the curriculum is delivered effectively; ensuring governors' policies and legislation are informed and implemented, and that information about the school is communicated to a wide range of audiences; directing LEA and community relations and overseeing all sorts of changes hitting the education world.

On 1996 figures, most heads are in their late forties to early fifties. On average, they have been in teaching for twenty years or more, and the vast majority (80 per cent) are male. The NAHT outlines a typical head as having experience in more than one school, with a minimum of three years at deputy head level. He or she would probably have teaching experience up to head of department or faculty level, and/or experience of a pastoral post such as head of school or year. The prospective head would have experience of operating beyond the confines of the school, for example in LEA-wide activities, and possess proven managerial qualities. Further qualifications in management would be desirable, as would a broad range of in-service training relevant to the post (which might include an MA in Educational Management, HEADLAMP courses resourced specifically by the TTA to train heads, and in future the NPQH itself). He or she would be paid according to the size of the school and possibly awarded a discretionary payment if the social, economic and cultural background of the pupils was a significant factor in his or her work. In return, the average head works a sixty-two-hour week.

The long hours are, according to Bob Lloyd, head of Hendon School, a 1,200-pupil grant-maintained comprehensive in North London, the only drawback of the job, although he does believe that the pressure (if not financial rewards) is pretty much in line with directors or institutional heads in other comparable fields.

Initially, I didn't plan to be a head, not until well into my career. I always knew I wanted to teach, not because of my experience of school, but quite the reverse – I thought I could do better than my teachers. I did a zoology degree, followed by postgraduate work, but then I had to start earning quickly so took up my first post. Because of circumstance, my route has therefore been the traditional school–university–school – I regret never having done anything else.

One's career is built so much on chance. My first job was in a grammar school, because that was what I was used to, but the quirk was that it was also a boarding school in the state sector. Whilst I was there I was appointed one of the resident housemasters. That was an important stage in my career, as for the first time I started to think broader than my subject. Despite the selective nature of the school academically, the intake was very mixed socially – some pupils were referred by social services, some were forces children and some were sent by parents who saw the school as a cheap independent – and I got involved in the pastoral side. By the early seventies, the move to comprehensives was happening all over the country and I felt I had to get experience of a wider ability range. I moved to a thirteen to eighteen upper school as Head of Biology, to a much more diverse ability range. This developed my interest in pedagogy. The school was working in a grammar-school tradition but with a much wider ability range, and so lots of current concerns were very real – differentiation, flexible teaching methods. I stayed four years.

What happened next was crucial, and again a chance development. The LEA I was working for went fully comprehensive, and my school combined with the local secondary modern. Suddenly, I was in my first big school, with the full age range, and the amalgamation meant that lots of jobs were re-advertised internally. From being in a deputy role in the Science department, I was catapulted into a senior management team job. At the age of twenty-nine I went from the equivalent of a two-responsibility-point job to a five-point job, as the senior teacher overseeing Years 10 and 11 (500 kids combined from the two schools) and two year heads. It was also a formative experience because I saw how badly that reorganisation was handled; I was convinced I could have managed it better. I suppose that's when I began to think about becoming a head.

My next move came after the two difficult years of changeover, to a deputy headship in an eleven to sixteen school. There was a minimal salary increase but the experience was significant. The school was new, but again, it was an amalgamation, and the management tasks were huge: two schools moving onto the site of a third, bringing in 900 children new to the site, under a new head, and a deputy who had been at neither school, whilst combining two 'old' staffs and newly appointed teachers! It was a nightmare, but challenging and valuable; it's important, I feel, not to avoid jobs because they aren't perfect. I always ask staff to have a go, as you can work with anyone in any post as long as you know it's just a stage in your career.

I was deputy in charge of curriculum for five years, and also took on a pastoral role during that time. It's important for deputy roles to be as wide-ranging as possible, to get the necessary experience for a headship. It also influenced my views of education. As far as I'm concerned, the pastoral system has to support access to the curriculum and here we combine pastoral and curriculum jobs at senior levels. I'm not a great believer in a divide between the two.

Unusually, my next move was to another deputy headship – few heads have experience of more than one deputy job. But I've found it immensely helpful. The job was a sideways move, but to a much bigger school (and salary!), and one with a huge building problem, where I was in charge of a £10m programme. So I added resources and accommodation management to my experience. This breadth of experience is the key to preparing for a headship, I think. I also wanted the chance to do things my own way, another reason why I'm a head. In my opinion, the three best jobs in education are head, head of department and class teacher, because you've got total control in all these, and very clear cut responsibilities. And not only did I have substantial experience of managing change, which is essential, but I enjoy change. I'm no good at 'if it ain't broke, don't fix it!' One of the things I've enjoyed about going GM is the freedom to get things done. I also like being a head because I'm in teaching to make a difference to kids – and you can do that most immediately as a head, or as a classroom teacher. I think I would have got bored eventually with being a classroom teacher, but it's crucial for a head to really enjoy being with children. I do.

Where do heads move on to? There used to be lots of options – inspection, LEA work, senior advising, TVEI management. These days, most have disappeared and most heads either move to a bigger school, or retire early and go into consultancy. From schools' points of view, it might be better if heads were moved around after five years, rather like senior civil servants, or as they do in some other countries; but from a purely selfish point of view, I'm happy where I am!

DEPUTY HEAD

According to the Secondary Heads Association's pamphlet on the role of the deputy, change is afoot: 'I welcome a move to a more professional and progressive role, away from the dogsbody image,' says one of their typical respondents. The head is accountable for all aspects of education in a school – so of course some duties have to be delegated, and the more the head's role has grown, the more fully some of these duties have been delegated. This is where the deputy comes in. Although not all deputies are would-be heads, the new-look deputy sees him or herself as a major contributor to school policy-making and management, and less an administrative support. The School Teachers' Pay and Conditions does too, which is why a very recently noted trend for cutting back on the number of deputies (to save money) has been roundly criticised. (A stereotype of the deputy job as pedestrian does still exist, however, possibly because 50 per cent of current deputies have been in their job for between five and fifteen years. Two heads of department summed up this rival view – 'I'm not interested in a deputy headship, all naughty kids and money' and 'You should be able to jump over the deputyship straight into a headship; the two jobs have nothing in common.')

The number of deputies in a school can vary – most commonly two – as do the duties they are assigned. Sometimes there is an official (or unofficial) 'first deputy' who is first in line to step in when the head is absent. Traditionally, there has been a curriculum and a pastoral deputy (although these two functions are increasingly combined in one person). 'Curriculum' jobs might include leading the curriculum committee, liaison with heads of department, monitoring curriculum development, and overseeing how the curriculum is delivered through the timetable and options. 'Pastoral' might include overseeing equal opportunities and special needs provision, and the discipline and reward system; liaison with pastoral heads and local primaries. A deputy's duties can also involve being responsible on a day-to-day basis for staff development and school INSET; finance and resources; governors' sub-committees which look at specific areas of concern; personal – including non-teaching staff – and recruitment; outside links and marketing of the school; health and safety. All deputies are likely to supervise middle management in some way. In order to develop senior staff, duties are often rotated and restructured between the deputies, to provide wider experience. Deputies work on average only five hours less than heads per week; like heads, they also have their own pay scale. Their deputising role is also more active, given that heads are now more frequently off-site.

THE SENIOR TEACHER

Most schools have three or four senior teachers, on the maximum five responsibility points (or old E allowance), who are responsible for an area of whole school planning or a significant policy issue. Areas of responsibility are usually neatly linked to year groups or particular tasks. For example, depending on the ethos and size of the school, there will be senior teachers in charge of Years 7–9 and Years 10–11 and the sixth form (called Heads of School or Key Stage Managers). Typical administrative or policy areas assigned to a senior teacher might be Assessment, Timetable and Cover, or

Exams Secretary; people jobs might include initial teacher training, NQT co-ordinator or teacher in charge of staff development.

As with deputies, the trickle-down effect of the changes in the head's role means that senior teachers are also catching crumbs from his or her table; it seems their numbers are increasing whilst deputy posts are decreasing. However, their remit will probably be more focused than a deputy's, and a senior teacher's job is not necessarily seen – yet – as a further step towards a headship. The post is therefore filled by all sorts of people, heading in divergent directions. Here are three examples:

I added points until I became Head of Maths. I did the job for four years before deciding it wasn't for me – I got it too young and it needs qualities I don't have (as well as some I do). Discipline was a problem and everyone else's discipline problems are yours too in that role. I was able to step down without loss of face – a plus point to the school – and was lucky in my next head of department who used my qualities well. I was offered the Examinations Secretary job three years ago and it was just what I needed. I like getting the detail right, and enjoy this kind of rigorous administration. My next step will be retirement, but gently, possibly via some part-time work.

I have changed direction all the time. First a pastoral job – as deputy head of house I started to see students holistically, and dealt with many educational partners. Then I was lucky to move into 'Unit' work for behavioural problems, and next co-ordinated GNVQ and CPVE, as well as careers guidance – vocational education lifts you out of a projectionist view of your subject, and teaches you to appreciate the need for the academic–pastoral divide to be healed. And now curriculum. As KS4 manager I enjoy the management experience, the staff contact and curricular development. I would like a deputy headship and possible headship – doing a good job and being recognised for doing so is important to me, as is working as a team.

My post title is curriculum co-ordinator. My responsibilities include curriculum, timetable, admissions, marketing, staff appointments, ITT reports, calendar, parents' evenings and the school's annual conference! I love dealing with people and the variety and the opportunity to get things done and follow ideas through, in a lovely school. But I'm also fed up with other local deputies telling me I'm doing more than any of them for less money. My headteacher is encouraging me to apply for headships but I feel I need to be a deputy first.

MIDDLE MANAGEMENT

Pastoral posts: Heads of Year or House

Curriculum Posts: Heads of Faculty/Alliance
– English, Maths, Science, Humanities, Modern Languages, Technology, Expressive Arts

Heads of Department
– Geography, History, RS, Home Economics, Design and Technology, Art, PE, Information Technology, Business Studies, Vocational Education, Special Needs

HEAD OF YEAR

Heads of year – or heads of house, if the pastoral system in a school works like this – are responsible for the general welfare and progress of a large group of children, typically about 200. They also lead the tutors who are in day-to-day contact with those children, and are the first point of contact for advice and action if a child has a problem the tutor can't deal with directly. They make sure staff are aware of children's domestic, health or learning circumstances, and consistent in the way they deal with such difficulties. Much of their work involves sorting out problems directly with children, but they also work with external agencies like educational welfare officers, youth counsellors, social services, educational psychologists, truancy officers and the police. Subject-specific problems are dealt with in the first instance by heads of department, but if a child is cause for concern or has special needs in all lessons, it will be the year head who steps in – they are interested in the general development and learning of the year group. The year head is a middle manager, probably with three responsibility points for his or her work. He or she is usually managed by a pastoral deputy head or senior teacher, and discusses school strategy with them. In turn, the year head manages a deputy.

Individual contact with children is a large part of the job, but so is the motivation and management of the whole year group – from behaviour to attendance, to sanctions and rewards, to homework policy, to year group extra-curricular activities, to arranging curricular choices, parents' evenings and reporting. Lastly, they will organise a PSHE programme appropriate to the year group, and be responsible for their spiritual and moral development.

The job is famously time-consuming, possibly because the year-head job is rather squeezed into the school structure. Pastoral heads and deputies are usually internal appointments and their work is crammed into the timetable, with little extra time and plenty of distractions from the interviews with pupils and parents which are at the heart of the job. 'I have empathy with disruptive, disturbed and unsuccessful students, and have success with them. Pastoral care has taught me to value all students' strengths. But the bureaucracy is a nightmare. Accountability is right and proper, but interference is not,' says one pastoral manager.

Ian Frost is Head of Year 9 at a Church of England School in London, a position he reached by the age of twenty-nine. He was always clear where his interests lay.

The teachers I respected in school were people, not guys standing at the front of the class trying to get their exam results. I am interested in children, not just teaching a subject – their problems and development and learning. My job is about problem solving. I love it when – working with parents and teachers – you can put your finger on what is going wrong with a child who is trouble in all his or her lessons, and find a solution. I have a school office where children will actually come and talk if they're in difficulties – I've got a battered sofa and a box of tissues for just that purpose!

In a school where the pastoral system is so strong, pupils are aware of him as an important figure, and parents 'see you as the teacher most responsible for their child's education'. A great deal of his job is information handling, and making sure that feedback happens effectively. 'If there's trouble at home, a kid's teachers have to know ... or if there's friction between particular students ... or a parent is concerned.' There is so much information circulating between parents, teachers and children that a year head must, he says, 'beware of becoming a messenger boy – you've got to remember what your own plans are in the midst of all this traffic'.

The other key area of his job is working with tutors:

> Managing a good team is great. When the difficulties come, it's because there are tutors who want to be with children, and tutors who want to be 'teachers'. In this school, the pastoral emphasis is a real strength, but it can be extremely difficult encouraging 'teachers' to engage with the kids in their form.

Particularly as children's development is intangible:

> I want to see kids taking responsibility for themselves, being honest, learning well. You can check a subject teacher's lesson plans and monitor their curricular work on paper, but checking a tutor's input to a child's growth is much harder.
>
> The worst aspect of the job is that you spend 80 to 90 per cent of your time dealing with the same five kids – you feel you're not reaching about 96 per cent of the kids in your year group. And pastoral work is exhausting, especially if staff tend to see you as the answer to all their problems. Here, we tend to steer away from that disciplinarian view of the year head; I don't want to be seen as 'The Shouter'. Instead, we are trying to be more curricular in our pastoral system, and one job I would like to do in the future is Head of School, looking at kids' learning. You can go back in on the curricular side and take with you all you've learnt in a pastoral role.

He reached his position two years ago, after two and a half years as deputy to 'a dynamic year head who grabbed me and made me apply for the job. I got lots of experience – lots of discipline, kids' problems – and I've been very lucky in my mentors. I'm also in the right place – my natural bent fits here.' As a Christian working in a church school, Ian enjoys being part of the community ethos, although he is glad of the mix of beliefs amongst the staff.

Christian values don't come through the daily acts of worship Ofsted insist on. They come through kids seeing teachers as role models, and learning decent behaviour and honesty by example. Kids like the camaraderie and good spirit they see between teachers; it leads to more openness.

His tip for a successful teaching career – particularly in pastoral positions – is to

put your personality into the job. When you're first starting out it's hard to have the confidence to do so, but don't put on a front – it's too stressful to maintain. Be honest with the kids and they'll always respond. They want to see that you have a life!

HEAD OF DEPARTMENT

I enjoy responsibility, decision making, making changes, motivating staff, pushing forward, raising standards and having an impact on the whole school.'

>   Head of Maths, formerly underwriter for insurance company

Along with the headteacher role, another post which has attracted much attention recently is the head of department. Subject-specific managers make up about 20 per cent of staff, but their visibility and autonomy put them in a clear 'box' – there is, after all, only one head of art or science in a school. The TTA have chosen to focus on 'subject leader' qualifications early on, in tandem with their work on headteachers and the classroom teacher. In the autumn of 1998, the National Professional Qualification for Subject Leaders is likely to appear. This qualification has much in common with the NPQH, and emphasises many areas of expertise found within headship training. The difference is that they are exercised within the narrower domain of a department, rather than a whole school. (Career development and national qualifications for other secondary-school 'leaders' who are without a subject-specific role, like year heads, are not yet planned, probably because their work is more diffuse.)

Heads of department have to monitor, evaluate and improve the work of their staff and pupils, manage a budget and resources, handle people, and take responsibility for teaching, learning and the curriculum. Like the head, the head of department is also obviously accountable – for the progression of pupils in their subject area, for staff, and for providing information to governors, parents and the senior management. Also like a head's job, there have been concerns that the head of department job is overloaded. An OUP study in 1995 said some HoDs felt that they were so snowed under with changes in the National Curriculum and exam syllabuses that they weren't free to engage in the managerial and overview tasks important to the school and also to their own careers. However, HoDs in large departments also felt their jobs were valuable in preparing them for more senior jobs, as they had experience of appointing and managing large teams, experience of change and devolved budgets, were involved in educational innovations, and were visible within the school structure.

A Head of Department post is likely to attract three or four scale points, depending on the size of department and school. Their line manager might be a head of faculty or alliance, and beyond that the deputy or deputies responsible for curricular matters. A deputy or deputies will support their work: a Head of Science would manage not only a deputy but heads of Chemistry, Physics and Biology; a Modern Languages head would lead deputies in charge of, say, Spanish, French and German; and a Head of English might manage a deputy and the heads of other smaller and related departments, like Media Studies or Drama. Lastly, and importantly, they will manage their departmental staff who – unlike pastoral heads and their 'staff' or tutors – they have a hand in employing.

Vicky Bishop, in her early forties, is Head of Geography at Lutterworth Upper School and Community College, a post she has held since 1986. The three main requirements for a good head of department are, she says 'enthusiasm, hard work and the ability to manage the team in an open style. You need to treat your team like the professionals they are, and discussion is crucial, even when there are hard decisions to be made.' As a member of the TTA's subject-leader working group she hopes that improved training for heads of department will follow. 'I would have appreciated the chance of a qualification – but I hope also it will help put more status back into the middle-management role. After all, it's the kids and their learning which is important, and as a head of department you have a huge effect on both.' The drawbacks of the job are 'dealing with budgets and mundane accounting'.

Her route to HoD began when she was given a point to take charge of Geology in her department. For a few years thereafter, 'things went quiet, but I couldn't move. Then my head of department went to do an MA, I became acting head, and kept the post when he returned to school.' Her enthusiasm for her subject and students is what drives her, outside school as well as in. She is a coursework and consortium moderator for GCSE, delivers exam board INSET, writes best-selling textbooks and is involved in the development of new A level syllabuses. 'I'm probably doing too much, but I get such a buzz from being involved that I can't stop. Mainly, I want to see the kids do well and enjoy my subject, and my job satisfaction comes from seeing excellent exam results, and the high take-up of Geography at A level here.'

Now at a crossroads in her career, she doesn't want to lose touch with classroom teaching, nor her subject. 'I want to make a difference in geographical education, but openings in teacher training and advisory work are limited. I was recently promoted to take charge of the initial training of student teachers based at Lutterworth though, and it's showing me I can enjoy work outside my subject area.' She is considering senior management: 'I've completed an MA in Curriculum and Management in Education. Another option is to become an Ofsted inspector, or in ten years I might simply be doing all the "extras" I do now full-time.' Her main advice to new teachers is to get involved. 'This is how opportunities come. One thing has always led to another in my career.'

OTHER POSTS OF RESPONSIBILITY

Careers and Work Experience
IT co-ordinator
Teacher in charge of Library

Deputy Heads of English, Maths and Science
Deputy Heads of Year

Heads of Spanish, French, German, Chemistry, Biology, Physics, E2L

Cross-curricular co-ordinators (e.g. citizenship, environment)

Duke of Edinburgh Awards or Community Work co-ordinator

How teachers get a single responsibility point or their first step on the ladder will vary. Whilst senior management posts can differ in their content, all schools have heads, deputy heads, year heads and department heads. But other posts of responsibility in teaching are a less rigid part of the structure. Posts attracting single or two points can be fixed deputy jobs; others depend on what areas are being developed within the school, the subject specialism and other, very localised factors. For example, responsibilities for doing the groundwork within a particular key stage (e.g. KS3 co-ordinator) or recurrent organisational jobs (e.g. arranging field trips) often carry two points. Or a point might go to the teacher in charge of the School Council, or the department's SENCO (special needs co-ordinator).

Some teachers uninterested in further promotion stick with these duties for a significant period, having found their niche. However, they are also an opportunity for aspiring managers to get first experience of those areas classroom teaching itself doesn't deliver (although some of the skills involved will be the same): teamwork, leading your colleagues, being responsible for planning, training or organising their work in a certain area, investigating legislation or syllabuses, formulation of policy, cross-department liaison or whole-school administrative responsibilities.

Secondary Education

Finally, these are the jobs which often come as a result of work instigated by an enthusiastic and interested member of staff. A head of modern languages advises: 'Don't expect to be promoted first and then deliver the goods. Make your mark in an area you can develop and enjoy and make sure you get noticed for it.' Initiative and a can-do attitude goes a long way in teaching (as in most jobs), and following your interests can lead to success. But a word of warning is probably in order too. Whilst a surly 'I'm not paid for that' outlook gets you nowhere and won't maximise your enjoyment of your career, a healthy self-respect is also in order. Schools are frequently strapped for cash, and with the best will in the world may end up stretching their staff's goodwill. Once you feel you are making a valuable contribution, bring it to your managers' attention, and suggest they reward you in return. Difficult though it may be to find someone else doing exactly the same as you somewhere else in the school, and being rewarded for it, the school should have some criteria for these first awards. Think also about how you can quantify the impact of what you do – the number of staff and children involved, impact on subject results or take-up by pupils, good PR with parents and the community. It's not just a financial matter – your CV will be helped by the status points given to your work.

5 Homework, and Leaving School

A steady and unbroken climb up the full-time ladder is not, of course, for everyone. There are plenty of teachers who haven't lost their enthusiasm but want to diversify the nature of their work, or who've come to a point in their careers when they want a rest from the classroom and a spell of other education-based work, or feel ready for a permanent move into a related field. This is not to mention career breaks taken – overwhelmingly by women – for family reasons, or changes in hours or working practices to accommodate young children. (A Scottish survey in 1992 found that the reason 40 per cent of teachers leave the profession is to care for children or other family members.) And, if surveys are to be believed, there are also plenty of disenchanted teachers who have had enough of teaching, and simply want out into a brand new field where they can use the skills they've developed in the classroom (11 per cent of leavers, according to the same research).

Teaching is probably no better or worse than other careers in how much movement or moonlighting it allows. It does, however, seem a shame that education isn't more willing to be flexible with its work-force, both for reasons of principle and pragmatism. Fresher teachers, able to pursue their own interests and enthusiasms, make for fresher lessons; more fluidity between the main jobs and phases in education would enrich all sectors; keeping and readmitting experienced teachers in the profession eases shortages and avoids wastage. More could be done in all of these areas; perhaps the General Teaching Council outlined in the White Paper will take up the cudgels on behalf of teachers' learning and wider experience.

Nevertheless there are people who mix and match activities which are linked to teaching, and some sidelines are easily accommodated into teachers' full-time working lives – for example, tutoring or examining. What seems to need a bit more luck is getting to operate in more than one sphere at once, but read on to see how some individuals have managed to carve out a little job flexibility and diversification for themselves, either temporarily or permanently.

PART-TIME AND JOB-SHARES

People want to work part-time for all sorts of reasons: to pursue other money-making activities, to fit in a course of study, or simply to make time for other interests – or people. There are about 12,000 part-timers working in secondary schools, and nearly 90 per cent of these are women. The NASUWT says that part-time work is becoming more widespread in the primary sector, but that the situation in secondary (although rising) can be less flexible. Teaching loads are not easily crammed into three neat days, given that it's unlikely all the lessons of all your classes are going to fall on those three consecutive days. Some part-timers therefore end up teaching hours which are scattered across the whole week. One senior teacher with a ten-month-old child says, 'You can end up paying for full-time child-care to cover part-time hours. So some women I know end up paying to work part-time, because they want to work and because they want to keep a foothold in the profession. It's mad – but they say it's worth it. Myself, as a teacher of sociology – a less common school subject – and in a management job, I had no choice but to return full time. Financial considerations aside, I would never have found that combination advertised on a part-time or job-share basis.'

Opportunities for flexible hours seem to depend mainly on being in the right place at the right time, or on encountering a sympathetic school management willing to be creative – there is still unofficial reluctance in many quarters. And to an extent, it would be unreasonable not to sympathise with the difficulties of your school's timetable; the logistics of matching up

1000 kids with fifty different teachers for the requisite number of hours are challenging, without the extra level of difficulty injected by part-time members of staff. Getting part-time work mainly depends on the need of the school to keep you on, or on you being convenient if a part-time teaching load emerges from the timetable. However, as an increasing number of schools seem to be able to organise part-time work, it is reasonable to approach your employer if this is what you want. The NASUWT says that, before going to the head, you should contact your local union association for advice and any literature they have (for example, policy documents, or advice leaflets such as the NASUWT's 'Conditions of Service Advice Manual'). You should also find out what local agreements and LEA policies there are on part-time work. You can then discuss these with your employer, and ask them to look at the possibilities.

Job-sharing can solve timetable difficulties, if your headteacher is receptive to this kind of arrangement. Job-share differs from part-time in that the contracts employ specific individuals as a unit: a single timetable is divided by two people who have to work very closely, sharing classes and therefore records, planning, marking – everything connected with their pupils' learning. They carve up the hours of the working week between them sensibly (avoiding some part-timers' scattered teaching time). A drawback with some contracts is that your job depends on the reliability and – in some circumstances – continuing employment of your job partner; if he or she leaves, the school must offer you the whole post full-time, or make 'reasonable' attempts to find a replacement. If you won't take the full-time job and they can't find a new half for you, your contract can be terminated.

But when job-shares are permitted, they can be extremely successful and so are worth pursuing, not least because they allow teachers to stay on the promotion ladder and in posts of responsibility. Given that most promoted positions are unsuited to part-time, job-share can be the answer, and some advertisements will carry the line that 'job-shares are welcome or considered'. About fifty LEAs have job-sharing policies, according to the NUT, and some run registers of teachers who are interested in job-share, so that individuals and schools can match up suitable partners; it's worth finding out whether your local LEA is one of these. It is unclear how widespread job-share is in practice; it depends on how open-minded school managements are in practice. An experienced teacher going for a head-of-department job-share encountered reluctance.

I had been out of the classroom in advisory work, and was ready to move back into mainstream education. Having left as an experienced second in department, and having spent the interim couple of years getting experience directly relevant to the head of department role, I linked with a teacher with a similar CV and we applied for job-shares. A job came up at my job-share partner's school, and she was invited to apply. So we did – as a pair – and weren't even short-listed. We each fitted the job specification exactly, she had been asked to apply alone – it was clearly a prejudice against job-share. The experience repeated itself too. As soon as we split and began to apply separately, we both got interviews. Looking back, we should have taken the case further.

In any negotiations regarding job-sharing or part-time work, it is worth staying in contact with your union over the terms of your particular situation; even the most fair-minded employer can fall foul of the complexities of these arrangements. Pitfalls to avoid are timetables which involve your non-employed (as opposed to your non-contact) time being spread across the week instead of being blocked sensibly; contracts which have you working 'half' the day – a morning or afternoon – when the two aren't usually equal in secondary timetables; job-shares where the share is not equal, or where there's no time given for liaison; changes of contract in the shift from full-time to part-time which may disadvantage you. Another source of information on job-share and flexible work is the organisation 'New Ways to Work', funded by the Equal Opportunities Commission amongst others. The London office advises individuals as well as employers on practical issues: contact 309 Upper Street, London N1 2TY or phone 0171 226 4026. If opportunities for more flexible working aren't forthcoming, it's not unreasonable to ask why. The school should have a rationale for refusing certain arrangements, and once you know their objections, you may be able to overcome them. (Even though part-time work is not a right, there have been cases of industrial tribunals finding in favour of the employee; limits on part-time opportunities are beginning to be seen as discriminatory, given that the vast majority of part-timers are women.)

SECONDMENTS AND CAREER BREAKS

As with any workers, a break of any significant time is bound to have an effect on the shape of a teaching career. Work-related breaks do happen, although not in great numbers – sabbaticals might be granted by a more enlightened head so that members of staff can pursue extra study, although the standard educational MA is usually achieved by part-time study over a number of years. One maths teacher with an enthusiasm for computers was released for two years by his independent school to ride the wave of the new technologies: 'The introduction of computers and calculators in the seventies gave me an enormous opportunity to write and publish articles, software and books.' He returned to head their IT department, and thirteen years later moved out into business as a systems manager, and then returned to teaching, moving to the state system as an 11–16 school's IT co-ordinator. It's worth seeing if your job would be held open for you, and you may well be in luck if your time out seems relevant – for example, the head of department who went off to get an MBA. However, time out is very much at the discretion of a head and governing body; and if circumstances change, they may not be able to hold to such agreements, and so it's worth getting arrangements in writing at the very least (and advice from your local association). A few LEAs have a 'right-to-return' policy for those wishing to leave the profession for a few years for family reasons – contact your LEA to see if yours does.

On rare occasions, secondments are also possibly to LEAs, inspection teams or research – these happen mainly at senior management level and can be advertised in the *TES*, *Guardian* Education section, LEA information and national press. These are instrumental in giving teachers a first step into advisory and consultancy work (see below), as they offer a much broader perspective than you can get from working within a few schools. For example, Nottinghamshire LEA recruit a handful of specialist advisory teachers through their vacancy bulletin, and currently have a teacher on secondment to an outdoor education centre, and to an environmental service project. All these are for fixed periods – usually twelve months – and teachers retain their teaching salary during their secondment.

Other work-related secondments can include managerial 'supply' on behalf of the LEA, who might wish to send a deputy in one of its schools to act as head in another borough school, if it cannot fill a vacancy; this is more likely to happen in the primary sector, but some opportunities do come through LEA head-hunting. One teacher took a 'roving' job in science departments across a London borough with subject shortages, filling head of department and straight teaching vacancies for an average of two terms. 'It was varied, stimulating, got me a variety of experience – and you could say truthfully on your CV that you had to be good to be able to do it. I got an advisory post after having done it.' Exchanges with teachers abroad are another option, and one you could instigate yourself (see chapter 6).

Barry Gandee of the NASUWT advises that any break where you are not coming back to a safeguarded job should preferably be taken early, 'while you've fewer experience salary points. You will still be cheap to employ when you return, yet will be able to offer extra experience. If you have more teaching years under your belt, you could go abroad – say as a head or a teacher trainer – and return to get a more senior position, still on the same points.'

On a more practical level, returning after a significant break needs some thought. To get back in, returners firstly need to build their own confidence. Supply and part-time work are both popular ways of doing so, and LEA refreshers, school observation, curriculum and syllabus reading, and contact with subject associations are also recommended to get you up to date. Pauline Buzzing's handbook, *An Effective Return to Secondary Teaching*, is a very helpful guide on what you can do to 'self-tutor' yourself in preparation for applications or a first post. Contact your LEA to see if it provides specific support for return teachers – some authorities like Kent and West Sussex have done ground-breaking work in this area. The NUT's 'Returner's Booklet' is also quite useful. TASC publish a pack 'Guiding you back: the teacher returner's A–Z', which includes a director of refresher courses, INSET and conversion courses provided by LEAs and teacher-training institutions.

However well-prepared you are and whatever career-enhancing study or experience your break has involved, you will most probably have to start again in the sort of post you left. For example, a teacher whose experience had prepared them for a promotion, but who decided to take a year out to do an MA, would have to come back in at the same level for a year (or more, depending how long the break had been), to consolidate before going for promotion. Your qualification and experience points are however safeguarded, which is where some returners encounter problems because of their expense compared with an NQT, given that teaching is at present a buyer's market. There was a suggestion by the last Government that returners might like to 'discount' themselves, by volunteering to drop their experience points. The STRB outlines the arguments against: 'We have been wary of the consequences of any relaxation of the existing position, and the teacher unions reiterated their opposition to any erosion ... of the principle that teachers should hold a minimum salary entitlement based on their previous experience. They said that the financial pressure on schools would place experienced teachers at a major disadvantage and at risk of being subjected to pressure and coercion.' A compromise position was reached whereby discretionary experience points (see chapter 3) could be surrendered by teachers moving schools or returning on a voluntary basis – but the NASUWT suggests you contact your union to see whether the school you are applying to has the budget to afford you at the 'higher rate'.

CASE STUDY

Nigel de Gruchy is General Secretary of the National Association of Schoolteachers/Union of Women Teachers. He began his career teaching English as a Foreign Language in France, before returning to London where he was Head of Economics at St Joseph's Academy for ten years. He joined the executive of the NASUWT in 1978, and moved to his present post in 1990.

I became a teacher in 1965 because it meant you could work with people, have a creative job and not have to suffer anyone looking over your shoulder and dictating every move you made. How that has changed! Coming to work in London at the end of 1968, I attended a union branch meeting to find out why teachers were not making more progress on their entirely reasonable demands for a fair deal on pay. My decision to attend that branch meeting of the then NAS in Lewisham was probably the most important one I made in my career. I got involved in a very lively discussion and within a few weeks found myself holding local office. I found teacher trade union work exhilarating.

I also enjoyed my early days in teaching enormously. However, by my mid-thirties I could see how much more difficult teaching was becoming. You had to put an enormous amount of energy into the job to make it a success. I judged that it was not a job for anyone over forty. I resolved by the time I attained the age of forty to be out of the classroom.

When I was thirty-five, having become the London Association secretary for NASUWT and having spent some three and a half years on the National Executive, I was lucky enough to secure a post that had become vacant in the recently re-established London office of the union. In that capacity, I began attending meetings of the national negotiating bodies, and representing the Association at national level. I also assumed the role of Press Officer.

In 1983 I became the Deputy General Secretary, and in 1990 the General Secretary. I anticipated nothing but blood, sweat, toil and tears. In practice, I have been delighted with some of the victories for NASUWT, although an enormous amount of work still needs to be done to raise the morale of teachers, and restore some decency to their professional lives.

DIFFERENT PHASES

Another option is to carry on full-time teaching but in a different phase of education. In theory, a PGCE qualifies you to teach all age groups. In practice, the shift from a secondary to FE is easy and requires no additional training – although you will have to be sure you are up to date with and preferably experienced in teaching a range of post-sixteen courses (see chapter 1). Moving to primary teaching is possible but you have to be aware of the huge differences in teaching and learning at that level, and the fact that you will be teaching all subjects, not just your own. A refresher or conversion course may be in order so contact your LEA and local training providers or colleges to see what your options are. A period of work experience in a primary will also be invaluable.

DIFFERENT PUPILS

You may want to step outside the mainstream completely, and start to teach pupils in less standard situations. The Association of Graduate Careers Advisory Services has an interesting little booklet called *Teaching: Beyond the Classroom* (£2.50, available from CSU Publications, Armstrong House, Oxford Road, Manchester M1 7ED) which raises all sorts of options – from teaching children in hospitals, to adults in prison, to travelling families, or in alternative education.

SUPPLY TEACHING

Supply can appear a thankless task. Called at 7.15 in the morning and told to be at the local hell hole by 8.30 a.m. to face they know not what, supply teachers have to be able to live with uncertainty. You're unlikely to know how much work you will get from day to day, what sort of classes you will deal with and whether you will get any information from the harassed staff around you. And you won't get a shoulder to cry on. Linda Karimi of the supply agency Recruit says that resilience is an essential quality. 'You might have had two really bad days in an unpleasant situation, but you need to be able to pick yourself up, ready to start again. Teachers need to be realistic about supply, and we are always honest with them so they don't get frustrated. You really have to be able to walk in and get on with it.' Warwickshire LEA personnel department add that stamina and good health are also key qualities, as the work is also seasonal – expect lots in germ-ridden Novembers and Februarys, but none in the summer, when teachers are healthy and do their own cover as exam classes depart and leave holes in their timetables.

So why do it at all? Some of the most enjoyable aspects of teaching – seeing kids develop, being part of a team – are denied the supply teacher, as well as those which make the job easier, like developing a rapport with classes and a knowledge of the ins and outs of the stock cupboard and referral system. What supply does offer, of course, is flexibility. Supply teachers can call the shots on how they work (within reason, as you will fare better if you aren't forever turning work away because you are only prepared to work very few days in very few areas, and refuse certain kinds of school). The work attracts all sorts of teachers, from NQTs to those with ten years' experience, and from all subject areas (although PE and food-technology teachers fare particularly well because their expertise is needed for practical lessons to go ahead). Frequently, supply appeals to young teachers who want to get some money together to travel, or to the newly retired who are equally uninterested in permanent contracts. LEAs are frequently more stringent with the teachers they will keep on their books (making police and medical checks, and excluding the over-65s and NQTs, the latter because, as Warwickshire says 'they need to be supported in a way which supply teachers are not').

Agencies offer a flat daily rate of about £80 a day; LEA pools pay pro rata according to your point on the scale, i.e. your experience. With agencies you don't get sick pay or holiday pay and are effectively self-employed; LEAs employ their supply teachers and arrange sick pay and pension payments (should staff want to opt into the superannuation scheme). Unlike primary supply, secondary doesn't involve providing the cover work for a class, so you can literally walk in with nothing apart from your emergency chalk; neither will you take home any marking or preparation, or have to attend meetings. It is a rare opportunity to experience teaching as an office-hours job.

For others, it is less a convenient and no-strings way of earning money, and more a reconnaissance mission. It can be a way for NQTs, unsure of what sort of school they are looking for, to work in all sorts of different localities and institutions. Or it can be the ideal way for teachers at the end of a career break to ease back into the classroom and gather confidence and information on what is going on in schools before trying for permanent posts. Long-term supply can be especially useful in providing a half-way house between the potential stresses of walking into the unknown on a daily basis, and making a strict commitment. Many schools have 'pet' cover staff whom they favour and keep in work more or less full-time, apart from the summer. (Some are also keen to use retired or resigning staff as supply teachers, as they have the obvious advantage of being familiar to staff and pupils.) The added bonus here – as with any extended contact with one school – is the possibility of a permanent teaching post coming your way as a result of your supply work.

Lil Llewelyn is a case in point. A history teacher with subsidiaries in English and drama, she taught in two schools before taking a long career break of ten years. She started supply work through a social contact; the local school secretary told her cover teachers were needed in a Reading secondary. She then moved to Surrey, signed up with the LEA list and worked in lots of secondaries. Another casual conversation at a rugby-club function led to regular half-a-day's cover for a teacher on union work, and when this finished, another member of staff at the same school conveniently broke his leg and provided a further twelve weeks' work. Her contact with this one school strengthened over seven years of supply, where she had worked in all her subject areas and in special needs (a personal interest), until she got three days' English teaching on a temporary contract. Her work at the school dried up, 'so I rang my local school and spent quite some time teaching typing! A history job came up for three days a week there and finally I went full time, with some drama. Now I fluctuate between history and drama, depending on how the kids choose in the option pools and where I'm needed.'

Having built a career on supply work, she attributes her success, firstly, to taking the job seriously.

It's no good just being a body in the classroom. I always explained the lesson, made sure they got some work done, checked homework. When I was on longer-term jobs, I volunteered to mark books and write reports, and you have to be versatile – I've taught just about everything. It pays to be proactive with the schools you want to work in – keep ringing them up and do a good job when you are with them. Finally, there's a bit of luck involved in being invited back – your face has to fit.

In return, she got a job which suited her family circumstances:

I'm willing and able to do full-time now – but it takes over your life. With supply, I could refuse work when I needed to. It allowed me to work wherever we moved, and saw me through the years when my children were growing up.

If you are interested in supply, look in the back of the *TES*, *Guardian* Education section and in your phone book for local agencies, and get in touch with your LEA personnel department who will put you on the register sent out to schools. (You will probably get better pay and benefits working for the LEA, but you may get more work through an agency, given that they stay open longer and therefore some schools go to them for a swift, round-the-clock service.) Finally, you can approach local schools direct, often a very effective way of getting work.

For further reading, Ann Cox is an experienced supply teacher who has written detailed and useful guides on supply. Her latest – *Your Guide to Supply Teaching* – is published by New Education Press.

TUTORING

Private tuition has a huge market. You don't of course have to have a PGCE to teach privately in a one-to-one situation, but most parents feel more comfortable with a trained teacher; working teachers are frequently asked to give extra lessons to individual pupils in return for payment. You may wish to tutor a child you already teach (although you should let your headteacher know, and be sure that it won't put you in a compromised position in the classroom). If you prefer not to mix your public and private practice, there are plenty of agencies advertising in the back of the *TES* and *Guardian Education*. Rates per hour can range from £15, and you will need to be able to get to your pupil's home. Most teachers tutor for extra cash, but some make a living from it when their reputation is established. One primary deputy head gave up her post as KS2 Co-ordinator to set up her own tutoring business, and has never looked back:

I was beginning to find classroom teaching stifling, and I was tired of being in endless meetings. Since I've been tutoring, I've got back to using my teaching skills, not my organisation, and the only admin I do is directly relevant to the needs of the children I teach. With my primary experience, and my B.Ed. in Maths, I teach the whole range of age and ability – from five year olds with special needs across the board, to competent mathematicians on A level courses: I teach about one-third primary and two-thirds secondary age. I have complete control and autonomy over my work, and I can meet my tutees' needs absolutely. I'm sitting beside them as they work their way through a maths problem, so I can catch them at precisely the point they get into difficulties. One-to-one is so relaxing, and I can see results very quickly. It's so easy to pitch the teaching at the right pace and level, so the children can really achieve, and I'm able to be very encouraging. As a result, I seem to keep my pupils for at least a year and I can see their development.

Her work comes mainly from word-of-mouth recommendations, and the contacts she made as a teacher and now as a tutor.

I have a permanent standard advert in the local paper but word-of-mouth is my main form of publicity. Private schools send a lot of work my way. I've also been recruited to do some home tuition, for children who are excluded; there's not a lot of this work around because of LEA funding shortages, but it's interesting and rewarding. It also provides work during the day, as otherwise tutors work very intensively in the early evening slot when children are home from school. The fact that you can't always spread your hours might not suit some people who are thinking about tutoring, but it gives me time to pursue my own interests during the day. I've also done a fair amount of part-time and supply during the day, which is essential when you are starting out. Once you're established, tutoring alone can bring in a good salary – say £20,000 a year – but when you begin you do need to supplement.

The work is more or less constant, partly because I think I've developed a positive reputation, and because I can offer a sought-after subject – science is also a big area – and general primary teaching skills. There are different 'seasons' – the run-up to GCSE and A level, the entrance exam period, and the term before the move to secondary school. I also have some permanent tutees, especially those with special needs.

I'm enjoying the work so much. I feel I'm able to be creative, and really teach. Teaching is such a flexible career – I don't understand why more people don't take advantage of this, to escape the routine of permanent school-based work. Yes, it's more risky (and I don't have to support dependants), but it's worked out extremely well. And I can see how other strands might develop here. Because I come into contact with so many teachers and they can see what I do, I've had lots of invitations to do Maths INSET, as well as actual job offers. And I really feel I wouldn't have trouble getting back into a permanent job; I could genuinely 'sell' this work as being very valuable CV material.

SPECIALIST SUPPORT TEACHING

For those looking for the one-to-one involvement that tutoring gives, but who wish to remain within an institutional and a professional career structure, there is specialist support teaching to consider. Support teachers work with individual children to support their statemented needs, either in mainstream classes, or in small group or one-to-one situations in a school unit. A class teacher can move into support work if they have suitable qualifications (e.g. SEN training undertaken as a subsidiary part of their PGCE) or on-the-job experience (teachers who are interested in this kind of work might get periods of support on their timetable). Teachers who are intent on pursuing their interest further can also get formal qualifications, via LEA INSET.

Louise Whittaker works for a local authority's Deaf Service, as a member of a specialist unit operating within a mainstream school. The school caters for pupils with all degrees of hearing loss – from slight to profound – with non-signing support. Louise came into support teaching after three years as a mainstream class teacher, having done a PGCE in History.

> I had come to the decision that teaching wasn't for me. I was frustrated with teaching a group of thirty. So much of the job seemed like police work, and not enough was focused on what I wanted to achieve with individual children.

By chance, she saw an advert for a job supporting primary school pupils with hearing loss. She applied, got the job, and underwent training within the Deaf Service; she has been working with hearing-impaired children ever since.

> I like the fact that the targets are more manageable – you can actually see results because you are working so closely with individual children. Seeing noticeable improvement is very motivating, and I also like the range of ability I get to deal with. As with a mainstream teacher, I can work with the least and most able, from the Year 7 curriculum up to A level support on a one-to-one basis.

Her unit colleagues are different in that they did an extra year on top of their PGCE course, training in technical audiology. Louise cannot, like them, make hearing assessments and maintain hearing-aid equipment; her lack of formal qualification also means that she is paid less and has less mobility within SEN work. (For example, she cannot sign, and would need to learn before being able to work in the vast majority of hearing-impairment special schools.) She is more focused on the learning needs of pupils with hearing loss:

> I'm trained in the particular challenges hearing-impaired children face in

terms of language acquisition. And I feel I'm doing what I do best, as I enjoy 'translating' classroom language in all subjects, simplifying and clarifying. Differentiation is also a large part of my job, which was also something I was interested in with my whole-class teaching, but didn't get the chance to do fully. Lastly, the job is more manageable than whole-class subject teaching. I may not have many options in terms of my career – getting the qualification I need would cost, and LEA grants are like gold dust – but it leaves me free to look after my children after school, and to get involved in extra-curricular activities, like the school expeditions I've helped lead.

Bob Barlow, Head of Central Support Services with Leicestershire LEA, says that Louise's case is fairly typical of mainstream teachers who have moved into SEN work.

There is a catch-22 situation at present, in that teachers interested in SEN work need qualifications to move into this area fully, but need experience to persuade grant providers to sponsor those qualifications. Something has to give. And, more and more, LEAs are arranging training on-the-job for interested teachers. For example, distance learning courses are a realistic option because the most expensive part of training is releasing and replacing staff. Training money is also being devolved to heads, so you may just be able to arrange INSET and funding at school level.

The profile of SEN has also been raised since the recent introduction of the teachers' code of practice, which points out that all teachers are teachers of SEN (as an estimated 20 per cent of children have special needs). This means that there is a greater awareness of such work, and more structured experience to be gained. Bob Barlow explains:

Teachers used to get into SEN work through very idiosyncratic routes. We do still place importance on potential, of course, and certainly take into account what we know of teachers we've seen working in mainstream classrooms. For example, interpersonal skills, communication and good classroom management are crucial in dealing with children who have emotional and behavioural difficulties. But now, the emphasis on SEN means there are opportunities for interested teachers to get experience in schools. For example, there are SENCO [special education needs co-ordinator] posts, and training programmes for SENCOs so that they can acquire the broad base of knowledge that they need. Our authority and the university are developing modular training for SENCOs which takes in assessments, record-keeping, literacy, dyslexia, working with other teachers, as well as training on specialist disabilities like autism.

Other institutions to contact if you are interested in further training are the education departments at Birmingham, Oxford, Manchester and Cambridge, which run courses, MAs and advanced diplomas in SEN.

Qualifications will also lead to wider career options and higher pay:

Most teachers working with central support services have a career path which is fairly limited – they mainly move from being unqualified to qualified, with some going into senior posts within the service or consultancy. Career paths are more defined in special schools – posts like Head of Department, curriculum co-ordinators and senior management posts are a possibility.

Pay for SEN teachers is on the teachers' pay spine as usual, except that all teachers who work for more than 50 per cent of their timetable with statemented children (i.e. those who have legally recognised special needs) get a one-point increment. Teachers qualified in shortage areas like autism, hearing and visual impairment will probably receive recruitment and retention points, and good qualifications attract points too.

EXAMINING

A way of becoming better informed about your curriculum and its assessment is to do some marking for an exam board. There are lots of different jobs involved in the education high season of May to September. Exam boards need plenty of markers who are willing to turn around papers at A level and GCSE in a fairly tight period in the summer (and the same, in smaller numbers, around the autumn re-sits). Preparation for the work usually involves some meetings with examination-board officials to get trained on the paper and do some trial marking. Moderators co-ordinate the work of markers, and also check schools' coursework marking – their 'live' period is more extended. Senior moderators are the next level up, checking the moderators' work and being involved in school visits, to standardise assessments or to iron out problems. Then there are the permanent staff employed by exam boards, who draw up syllabuses, train teachers, liaise with national bodies, set and review papers and oversee the whole examining process.

For temporary, seasonal examining work, you should contact the exam boards for application forms, experience needed, work schedules and pay – these will be different according to different subjects and papers, and whether there are shortages of markers. For example, a NEAB English Literature marker will be expected to have two years' recent teaching experience, to mark about 600 scripts in a three-week period and earn £1.96 per script. All examining work is likely to require a degree in the subject, very recent teaching experience and the vast majority are serving teachers doing the work as an extra. Senior examiners and moderators are likely to have had experience of relevant examining jobs, from marking upwards. SCAA also employ teachers as markers for the Key Stage 3 tests, which happen a little earlier in May. The money can be useful, but the involvement in the examining process is also good CV material, and enlightening.

TRAINING AND ADVISORY WORK

Advisory teachers are employed by LEAs as experts in their field who can support the work of teachers in local schools. They must have a good range of teaching experience, experience of curriculum development, and are usually expected to have managed and worked in teams successfully. They need to be full of ideas, good collaborators, and able to lead the specialists who will look to them for guidance and information. Salaries begin at around the £30,000 mark, for subject or age-range specialists, and rise for general advisers able to bring cross-disciplinary experience to the job, or those with experience of more than one age range. Their numbers have been diminishing, due to cut-backs in local authorities, and the fact that schools were given control of their own budgets under LMS, or because they became grant-maintained; the services of the adviser often became optional or prey to more pressing financial needs. There is speculation that this trend will be reversed. With a new emphasis on raising standards through developing teachers' skills, advice on good classroom practice will be needed.

Advisory work is also delivered increasingly by educational consultancy, as schools buy in their own training and LEAs cut back on their own INSET providers. There are ex-teachers acting as freelance consultants on all aspects of schools' work; most are ex-heads or at the least senior school managers, and most have had some kind of employment which has given them experience beyond a single-school setting. This might mean a spell working for an LEA, as well as training experience, and expertise in a specific area of education. Careful research is recommended in order to find out what the market needs in the way of training, and then consultants get their work from the kind of varied sources you would expect for freelance work, with word-of-mouth recommendation being one of the most important (another reason why senior teachers, with their years of contacts, are those most likely to be successful). Basic business know-how is needed, as well as the skills shared with teaching – the ability to communicate, plan and tailor training sessions to the needs of the trainees. Training ranges from one-to-one sessions up to whole-school workshop days. The work is lucrative (£300+ per day) but consultants need to cover the costs of being self-employed. There is an advice and information service called the Society of Education Consultants (contact Rita Russell, 256 Longfellow Road, Coventry CV2 5JH; tel. 01203 442701).

Like an adviser, the teacher trainer needs to be the expert's expert and will need to have similar experience – exemplary and enthusiastic classroom practice, and leadership skills. They will also need a higher degree of some description, and at least the potential to research and publish at a university level. The trainer needs to ensure that students can teach; the vast majority of the job is still training and supporting student teachers, in college and at teaching practice schools. Mick Saunders is Director of PGCEs at Nottingham University, and says, 'I wanted to be a teacher and that remains. Even though teacher education has become much more bureaucratic and administrative, teacher training has kept me in touch with teaching and learning, and given me another career path which didn't have to involve school management.' As well as teaching students, Mick supervises research, does his own research and is – to a large degree in his current post – involved in course administration. He is happy with his lot and is looking forward to continuing in teaching; other colleagues, he says, might see their future more in academia. 'There are openings in the area of research and publication; some people want to concentrate on building a national and international profile in teacher education – although a professor of education is (rightly, in my opinion) paid less than a headteacher!'

Bethan Marshall has been involved in a whole gamut of education jobs. An English specialist, she taught in three schools for her first nine years, and was Deputy Head of English and Head of Media Studies when she went on maternity leave.

I was ready for a break from the classroom, so I took a part-time teacher-training post at King's College London during my leave. This contract was renewed and at the same time my adviser and mentor at my old LEA rang to say that a two-day adviser post was in the offing. I had the equivalent of a full-time post, and took the opportunity.

In advisory work, what I really enjoyed doing was the research and development work, which came out of the idea of the adviser as someone employed to encourage good teaching in local schools. I would go into a school and work on a major area of the English curriculum – say, writing short stories – or a new teaching requirement which teachers had little time to work on themselves, as when more pre-twentieth-century literature needed to be included in schemes of work. I researched new materials, and team-taught them so that they got properly trialled in real classrooms. Once we were satisfied they worked, I published them and circulated them to other English departments in the LEA so they could use them too.

The adviser's role is also to make sure teachers understand new developments affecting their work and to support new teachers.

However, these important areas of advising have shrunk, as schools became more self-governing and isolated in my borough. I found myself working on tasks I enjoyed less and found frustrating. I was called in increasingly to inspect rather than work with teachers, and often this meant sitting in on lessons taken by failing teachers who hadn't been able to respond to their school's help, or to observe the work of beginning teachers rather than provide training and opportunities for them to meet. So, I decided to resign and concentrate my energies on teacher training.

Another string was soon added to her bow.

I got into educational journalism via campaigning against KS3 tests. It was 1991 and there were a number of emergent education issues hitting the headlines. I got some leaked information and rang the *Independent*, where the educational editor said, 'If you can make it 800 words long and jargon-free, I'll see about printing it.' I thought I'd been admirably clear and read it to a friend who said she couldn't understand a word. I tried to imagine my father trying to read it and that did the trick. The piece got printed, and I continued to cover issues for the paper and for the *Guardian*, the paper for which I now write most regularly.

TV appearances began with the debate about reducing coursework at GCSE.

Through campaigning, I got a profile, but I think it's really important that the education debate should be widened and popularised by people who know what's going on in the classroom.

She sees her future building on this variety of experience.

I've been out of straight classroom teaching long enough for it to be difficult to be re-admitted. I wish there was more fluidity and movement of individuals between the different sectors – primary and secondary, advising, teacher training – but cuts have led to more entrenched attitudes.

Teacher training offers the most interesting scope for her wide experiences and enthusiasms so she wants to continue at King's.

It is a five-star-rated department. Research is considered very important and I have plenty of opportunities to write. Directing MA work is satisfying as the classes are big and it feels like being in the classroom. Even though I'm dealing with adults, I get the same satisfaction of developing a rapport with a large group. And the fact that the MA students are experienced teachers means I can't become too impractical and wild in my research, which can happen in academia – they constantly hone what you are doing. So, combined with the initial teacher training, it's a nice mix.

INSPECTION

Advisory teachers are involved in inspection, but the major employer here is Ofsted (Office for Standards in Education). Or rather, indirect employer – inspections are contracted out to bidding organisations, who make up their teams from freelancers. Like consultancy work, this can be financially rewarding, depending on how much work you get and the fees paid by the different inspection organisations. There are two types of inspectors – team and registered – but both will have teaching experience, and experience beyond class teaching, e.g. senior management, advising, inspection, teacher training. The team inspector is a subject inspector, or inspects a whole school aspect, like management or teaching. The registered inspector leads the whole team. Both types need to be able to plan and manage inspection work, have relevant professional knowledge, and be good oral and written communicators. Training is part distance and part tutorial, and now it costs money – £900 for team inspection training, and also fees if you want training to cover a school phase or SEN. In 1997/8, no new registered inspectors were being accepted as they've got plenty, and in general the secondary inspection market is well served and therefore highly competitive.

TEXTBOOK WRITING

When I go to parties and people ask me what I do, if I say I'm a biology teacher their eyes glaze over and they want to talk about something else, but if I mention my books, then they're terribly interested. So I tend to say I'm a biology teacher.

Hilary Compton writes textbooks for the GNVQ course in Health and Social Studies, something she says lots of fellow teachers envy her for.

So many people have this image of sitting at home at a WP, tapping away by an open window, having retired from the stresses of the classroom. But it's quite different. For a start, I feel you have to be teaching in order to write well. When I'm thinking about activities to have in the series, I always have in my mind my current GNVQ class, and I write for them. If I can, I trial the materials with them. It's very important to know your audience, and that means being in contact with them; writing for a seventeen year old is not the same as for an adult.

She says it is important for aspiring writers to plan their writing time carefully. Working part-time at a tertiary college means that her writing at present is slotted around teaching and childcare, mainly in the evenings.

Now I have two children, it has become much more difficult to find clear time to write, and I am going to have to make proper arrangements to do it. I've tried working in the day with them around, and it's been a disaster. There have been times when I've been at the WP whilst my youngest son is waking, shaking the bars of his cot whilst I rush to finish the last paragraph. Working at home is not possible unless they are out of the way. I have to say that I find it very difficult to get started at the end of the day, but I don't want to give it up. It's an odd mixture of a burden and a pleasure – but once I'm started, I really enjoy it. I get tremendous satisfaction from seeing the books in print, although to be honest, lots of teachers could do it. My books are really no more than a set of lessons notes, except that you have to be bang up-to-date and 100 per cent accurate with your information.

My break into writing wasn't conventional. Normally, if you have an idea for a textbook, you draw up a proposal which covers the gap in the market your book would fill, the nature of the competition, the content and audience of your book and an idea of how many people might buy it. Then you send your proposal to an educational editor who deals with your subject area, who might commission it. My colleagues and I at the college were just lucky. We'd been teaching on the BTEC course when it had first come out. A Hodder editor came in on a visit and asked us whether we would buy a textbook to support the course teaching if there was one. We said yes – it was something we'd talked about in the department. So I asked whether they had anyone to write it. They hadn't, so we said we'd do it!

But don't give up the day job! Financially, the rewards are not great – I get £1000 here and there from royalties. There are a few authors writing for established courses with huge student numbers who do make a living from it, but that's unusual. I have done some writing for a Health Trust as a spin-off but apart from enjoying the writing, I see it as a form of personal development for when I go back full time. It has already led to other things. For example, because I needed to be so up-to-date with the course, I did a qualification which is needed for teaching GNVQ much earlier than most teachers. So I've been given the job of training fellow teachers. In the future, I hope to move into management, or perhaps into vocational education jobs elsewhere, and the writing is helping my CV.

OTHER CAREERS

Clearly, it would be impossible to list all the other careers you might go into if you wanted to leave the profession completely, as they are as varied as the individuals pursuing them – from the head of English at a highly respected girls' school who jacked it all in to drive a taxi, to the band of ex-teachers who joined Parliament as MPs in May 1997. The good news is that teaching clearly gives you some marketable, transferable skills and proves your competence in areas which many employers value – communication and inter-personal skills, organisation, management and motivation are the most obvious. For this reason, if you discover, having qualified, that teaching is not for you, your PGCE won't be wasted (as long as you don't give the impression that you did it on the off-chance and are now drifting on to the next professional port-of-call). If you've got some teaching years under your belt, so much the better.

There are some careers where recruitment is directed specifically at ex- or would-be ex-teachers. Education officers with charities, museums and other organisations with an interest in education are likely to be ex-teachers. Educational publishing is another (see the case study below). Beyond that, the picture is too broad to cover here, and it's worth contacting your local careers office for some advice, and browsing the job columns to see who's looking for which skills. *Teaching: Beyond the Classroom*, mentioned above, has some helpful suggestions, as might the COIC book *What can teachers do except teach?* by Barbara Onslow (a 1983 production, and therefore outdated, but it might trigger a new thought). There's also a book called *Moving on from teaching*, by Caroline Elton (published by Kogan Page), with a useful, guided self-assessment section which leads you through an analysis of your own skills before you go off on a job/retraining hunt. Here's the history of one ex-teacher:

I wasn't very good at teaching – teenagers and I didn't get on. In the same class you'd get thirteen-year-old girls going on twenty-one and thirteen-year-old boys going on seven and I didn't know what to do with them. I lost my temper too quickly, and felt dwarfed by these huge year 10s – all I could see were massive shoulders and boots, when in fact of course they were terribly awkward and shy. They could be so juvenile, and yet their ideas were great. Teenagers are merciless in their thinking, and don't namby-pamby around in the grey areas. That's really interesting, but I was still having to spend loads of time keeping people in their seats. I quickly decided it wasn't for me. After all, my original intention had been to do the PGCE in order to go abroad, and that's what I did.

First I went to Spain as a language assistant, and then to teach English in Colombia, which was an extraordinary culture shock. I enjoyed teaching the adults very much but cheating was really rampant and I was still too young to accept that cultural difference. I got into an absurd tugging match with one of my students during an exam; I finally wrestled his dictionary away to find all his notes written out inside. Coming from England – where people queued, didn't stay up until three in the morning, did things nicely – I disqualified him. The whole exam hall erupted into 'Oh Tanya, don't be so mean!', 'Tanya, be a sport!'

Bogota was exhilarating but I didn't want to be out of England for too long – it can get too difficult to re-establish yourself, get a job, afford a flat.

I got home and didn't have any idea of what to do next. I did do some refugee teaching; it's a real challenge teaching adults for whom literacy is the problem, rather than English. As with teaching in Colombia, getting back to first principles is a really good way to teach – in Bogota, I had a blackboard and, glamorously, a tape recorder, and one textbook, so you have to be inventive. I did an isometric test which said I should consider marketing, personnel and editorial. I'd never thought about the latter, and realised that I had the right qualifications and interests to move into educational publishing. I got my job commissioning EFL textbooks through the *Bookseller* – sign up authors from FE colleges, go to Spain and Latin America to research the markets and visit teachers, edit manuscripts, brief reps. I really enjoy it.

I think that everyone should do some teaching at some point in their life. It trains you to do so much – organising yourself, presenting information, explanation – which is valuable in business and elsewhere. And it has the satisfaction of being immensely intense, yet finite. A lesson ends and you get feedback, the year ends and your classes move on, whereas in other lines of work things rumble on half finished. I'm also glad that I did a PGCE, rather than EFL training. It taught me to plan lessons, time myself, think about different teaching methods – it felt like a more stable grounding.

Blackboards Abroad

According to a 1996 survey of student destinations, 2 per cent of newly qualified teachers head off overseas to begin their careers, but it is possible to find some way of using your teaching skills abroad at any time. There are some limits on your options – what you've got to offer in the way of subject, experience and qualifications, and how footloose and dependants-free you are – but if you're intent on going, there's probably a suitable opening for you.

The opportunities are numerous and varied, so this section merely provides an outline of the more frequently travelled paths to foreign shores. For more detail and less obvious routes, the Central Bureau for Educational Visits and Exchanges are the experts. They publish a whole book on the subject, called *Teach Abroad* (£8.99), which gives profiles of the teaching options in individual countries and details of the organisations involved in education abroad. They are also the publishers of two other useful publications: for temporary work, look in *Working Holidays* (updated in November for the next year), and for opportunities in a year off between school and higher education, there is *A Year Between*. These last two deal with all employment fields but include teaching, and might offer some good work experience if you're just testing the educational waters to see if you like being in a classroom situation or working with young people.

TEACHER EXCHANGE

This is one scheme where you get a real taste of living and working in a foreign country, without having to do any drastic bridge-burning. If you're looking for a temporary change to your working life, a teacher exchange might be just the thing to put a spring back into your step when you walk into your classroom a year later armed with your new experience, contacts and teaching materials. Administered by the Central Bureau, one scheme involves a direct exchange with a colleague overseas who teaches the same subject as you; you literally swap professional lives for a year or less, on the same pay. (Some preliminary visits and return travel are paid for, and year exchanges are eligible for tax relief.) The Bureau sees it as a 'cost-effective form of In-Service Training', given that schools benefit from a foreign teacher's input and neither institution has to lose a member of staff. It is a way of exposing yourself to new teaching environments, methods, and content, and a means to boost your own confidence in your skills and flexibility. The experience can also help you on your way to a new qualification – Newcastle and Southampton Universities, for example, accredit a European language exchange towards an M.Ed. or M.Phil. Finally, there is something of an ambassadorial role involved, as with volunteer work, so the organising institutions encourage applicants to be clear about their motives for exchange.

Exchanges are possible in the United States, Austria, Belgium, Denmark, France, Germany, Italy, Spain and Switzerland for various lengths of time. You can exchange for an academic year in all those countries except Italy and Belgium. The United States also offers a two-term spring and/or summer swap, or you could spend a single or half term in Denmark, France, Germany, Spain or Switzerland. The League for the Exchange of Commonwealth Teachers (LECT) operates a similar scheme between the UK and countries like Australia, Bangladesh, Canada, India, Jamaica, Kenya, New Zealand, Pakistan and Trinidad, with most LECT programmes lasting an academic year. (There is also some flexibility if you've already got a contact abroad in another non-Commonwealth country, and would like to organise your own exchange – contact the Bureau with your proposal.) Here's one exchange which went well:

My husband and I had always wanted to teach in the States, and in 1984–85 we did it. It was touch and go whether we would find exchange partners – asking for another married couple, both English teachers, to exchange with was quite a tall order, and the Bureau's first match for us fell through. But then in July we got a phone call with a contact. It gave us a month to pack up our family and our lives, and get our house ready for our American replacements. We went to Montana, and it was a match made in heaven. All the other exchange teachers we met coming back from the West thought theirs was the best exchange ever, too, which probably says something for America and Americans.

I taught at Big Sky High School – Montana's known as the 'big sky state' – and my husband at Hellgate, after the chasm at whose mouth the school stood. Educationally and socially, we had a tremendous year. Teaching in the States is so much easier in some ways: the students know they have to graduate to stand a chance in the employment market, but also that anyone can graduate if they work. They just have to get those assignments in – it's their responsibility. Their sense of loyalty to their school is so strong because everyone does something after class – cheerleading, debating, sports.

I went thinking I would spend a year learning about the American education system, but in fact what I thought about was the English education system. Everything about the way schools are run here came into focus. And, similarly, it wasn't until I got back to England that I began to understand the American system.

The year was just a catalyst. We've kept in contact with so many friends, and believe me, people would pay to have Montana friends – they're charming, warm, considerate, interesting. The learning in professional terms only began then, too; I still have access to American teachers' ideas, materials and literature through the colleagues I worked with. It hasn't made any difference whatsoever to my career, although I was asked about it at interview for my current [head of department] post. But it is still making a huge difference to my life, and to my teaching.

To qualify for an exchange, you need to be able to take over the basic teaching programme and other activities of your

exchange partner. (The Bureau warns that most managerial positions are therefore inappropriate swaps – if you have these kind of responsibilities, your school will have to shift them over to a colleague in your absence.) Most exchanges are between language teachers who, says the Bureau, have at least two years' teaching experience. The British teacher will usually be taking over a full timetable of English, and updating his or her language skills and cultural understanding, as well as setting up opportunities for student links and curriculum development. However, if you are a teacher of another subject, you could participate in an exchange if your language level is up to conducting lessons, dealing with students and working with staff and parents. Or you may wish to consider a Commonwealth exchange, or Denmark and the Netherlands, where you don't have to be a native language speaker. The less eclectic your timetable, the better, too; if you teach politics, SEN and some PE, then the organisers will be hard pressed to find you a twin overseas! Applications for exchanges with US teachers close at the end of November, and the European deadline is the end of January. Contact the Central Bureau, which has offices in England, Scotland and Northern Ireland, for further details and application forms in good time for these deadlines, as paper work will need to be attended to by your LEA or governors, as well as your own headteacher.

LECT applications are handled all year long; again, think ahead, as placements can take up to a year to arrange. Applicants are normally between twenty-five and forty-five years of age and must have five years' experience at the least, ideally the last two with the present employer. LECT publishes a very useful range of publications for exchange teachers, including its *Annual Handbook for the Use of British Teachers Applying for Exchange*, the 'House and School' booklet, a *Headteacher Information Handbook*, and a Study Project Resource Pack, listing the projects produced by exchange teachers. It also produced *Commonwealth Times*, a bi-annual magazine for exchange teachers.

If a year is too long, there is also an exchange scheme between the UK and European countries lasting three to four weeks, where language teachers carry out a joint project with staff and pupils designed to enrich the curriculum. Contact the Central Bureau if you are interested, asking for the European Post-to-Post Scheme.

NON-EXCHANGE TEACHING POSTS

For a unilateral move abroad but one which would still build on your teaching career, you might want to consider openings with the British Council. The Council needs all sorts of educational professionals to work in a wide range of institutions abroad: secondary schools, teacher training colleges, technical colleges and universities. Advisers are in demand in the areas of education, TEFL, teacher training and curriculum development, but for all posts, the Council prefers teachers with substantial experience, postgraduate qualifications like MAs, and some overseas experience. There are also posts in foreign government projects and ministries. If you feel this sounds up your street, contact the British Council's Central Management of Direct Teaching (10 Spring Gardens, London SW1A 2BN; tel. 0171 389 4931) for TEFL teaching posts in British Council centres, and its Overseas Education Appointments Department (Medlock Street, Manchester M15 4AA) for other posts.

Another possibility, but closer to home, is to teach in a European School. These schools serve the children of civil servants working in the EU, and are located in Belgium, Germany, Italy, Luxembourg, and the Netherlands, as well as in the UK itself. Appointments are filled in the New Year, and can last for a maximum of two four-year contracts (after a probationary year). The kind of recruit they are looking for has at least five years' experience, and a good working knowledge of at least one other EC language, as pupils are taught in their own and a second language. Write to the DfEE (European Schools section) for details.

VOLUNTARY TEACHING

Volunteer teaching isn't completely unpaid, but is so-called because of its humanitarian intentions. If you work abroad for

VSO, one of the Christian organisations or a charity, you will be contributing to their aid to developing countries; the sharing of skills with local people is the main focus, so that native teachers can be trained to replace you. As well as teaching at every level, there is much scope for teacher training and curriculum development. The Central Bureau's view is 'As a volunteer, you should be prepared for a more demanding post than perhaps you have been used to', but also 'that the ability to take on and cope with such extra responsibilities is always going to be an asset on any CV'. Demand areas include TEFL, maths and science, commerce and home economics, as well as SEN teaching of pupils with disabilities. Volunteer teachers therefore need to be flexible and resourceful, and willing to stay for around two years. They are paid a salary at local rates, and provided with accommodation and air fares.

The Central Bureau publishes *Volunteer Work*, and Vacation Work (9 Park End Street, Oxford OX1 1HJ; tel. 01865 241978) publishes two directories of voluntary work opportunities in the Third World and abroad. For details of schemes run by the various charitable organisations, contact them direct. VSO can be contacted through its Enquiries Unit, 317 Putney Bridge Road, London SW15 2PN; tel. 0181 780 2266.

TEACHING ENGLISH ABROAD

If you are prepared to be subject-specific, then teaching English provides numerous openings. The drawback here is that you will be somewhat limited if you want to rely on a PGCE and your own fluency in the language. A TEFL (Teaching English as a Second Language) qualification is almost essential, although there are possibilities of work for unqualified teachers (see below). Qualifications not only expand your opportunities of work, but offer you greater employment rights too; terms and conditions are better if you have formal TEFL training, and as most reputable institutions insist on it, you are automatically raising your chances of a decent post. Your bible should be *The English Language Teaching Guide: The Definitive Guide to Teaching English as a*

Foreign Language (published by EFL Ltd, see Appendix A for address), which is clear and exhaustive on what's available.

TEFL teaching is generally a young person's pursuit. The attractions are obvious, but for most this field isn't going to offer much job security – the pay is adequate, and the contracts short. There is much more likelihood of a career structure if you work for the large organisations, like the British Council and International House. For example, International House has exacting standards (you have to pass the Certificate with at least a B grade), and in return offers decent employment and the possibility of promotion within its organisation and schools.

The main qualifications for teaching English abroad are the RSA/Cambridge TEFL Certificate and Diploma, and the Trinity College TESOL Certificate. The Certificate is a practical course, dealing with students from beginners to late intermediate. You are taught language-teaching techniques, and encouraged to look at the learning process from the students' viewpoint, taking in their cultural as well as their learning needs. The course is intensive, in the case of the RSA running full-time for four weeks of six hours a day, or eleven weeks part-time (three hours a night, twice a week, or six full Saturdays.) Teaching practice is important – you work in small groups to teach classes at different levels, and therefore have to be a good team-worker as well as developing your own language-teaching skills. Observation of your lessons takes place in addition to the course hours, as do various extra-curricular talks and seminars. The full-time courses cost between £700 and £900, the part-time about £1000, and whilst a proportion of distance learning is available on the Trinity College certificate, the courses must be followed at a centre. Selection is based on a sound educational background, such as a first degree, the fluency of an educated speaker, and some experience of learning languages yourself. You must be at least twenty years of age. Applications involve a written form and interview, and you are encouraged to apply at least two months in advance of the starting date you want, as competition is keen. Find out where the nearest training centre is by contacting the RSA and Trinity College, who will also advise you about their respective course content and assessment.

Teachers interested in a career in TEFL – rather than an interesting but brief period abroad – may well want to go on to get the Diploma, which will open up more opportunities and senior posts. The Diploma is a full-time course, lasting twice the length of the certificate, and costing about £1300 in fees. You generally have to be twenty-one, already hold the Certificate, and have a minimum of two years' experience at a wide range of teaching levels. For TEFL teachers who are abroad, there is a distance training programme available, leading to the Diploma. Assessment is by practical and written examinations.

Clare Black sees her experience of TEFL as fairly typical,

in that I fell into it, but unusual in that I didn't do it because I wanted to travel. I had been in tourism for four years since leaving university with a languages degree, and I didn't want to be living out of a suitcase at fifty. I'd come back to England and was working as a travel co-ordinator with Regent Language Training Summer School, and didn't have a clue what to do next. The Language School TEFL department was three flights down, and someone suggested I went and had a look. As it wasn't far, I did, and ended up enrolling on a course – the path of least resistance!

She came out with the RSA certificate and despite her sought-after B grade, found herself caught in a common TEFL circle – no experience means no job means no experience. When a friend in Hong Kong suggested she try working there, she went, clutching a contact name in the British Council, for whom she began teaching children and adults part-time.

The British Council is an excellent employer. Their support system is excellent, their appraisal of teachers is very thorough, they pay well and they have all the resources and lesson plans you'd ever need. It was just what I needed, as a beginner. The only downside was temporary short-term contracts, depending on the numbers of students enrolling. My last job was on a joint British Council/Hong Kong Government project, teaching secondary-age pupils English so they could enter English-medium tertiary education. The students were very motivated and it gave me such pleasure when they improved enough to get onto their courses.

She then returned home, to have another go at establishing a career.

I swore blind I'd never be a teacher, especially when people assumed my modern languages degree was pointing me in that direction. But I was thwarted by a phone call. On the recommendation of a colleague at the Language School, I was invited to an interview for an English-as-a-second-language job in London's International School [one of fourteen privately run secondary schools in Britain, catering for students from across the globe]. Despite my vow, I went to the interview and as soon as I got there, I loved it; I've been here ever since. The staffroom was buzzing with all this international banter ... I love the cultural and linguistic mix of the staff and students – Spanish here, Portuguese there, Arabic, you name it. Yesterday at work I learnt that in Portugal a bounced cheque is called a 'ghost' cheque, and that the Japanese don't have an equivalent phrase because they can't conceive of anyone doing such a thing!

Clare's ESOL teaching in Britain began with a part-time post at the International School, running concurrently with another part-time post teaching refugees in Lambeth.

The contrast was a bit shocking. I'd come from a small class of very privileged kids, to find one of my adult students apologising for the fact that he wasn't going to be in class because the Home Office were about to deport him.

Eventually she joined the school's staff four days a week:

Fate had played its part all along the way, and here I was, a teacher after all. Then my boss left for Marbella, and suddenly I wasn't just a teacher, but head of the TEFL department to boot.

She enjoys the managerial role and the progress of her own students.

The best part of a class for me is when the children learn from each other, not just about English but about life in Madrid or Tokyo. That's the really unique buzz you get from TEFL.

The unqualified route is less organised and secure in terms of contract, wages and conditions, but it is possible. Some summer schools in the UK, and language schools in Europe, will consider PGCE-trained tutors without EFL training; it helps a great deal to have a European language. Some chains of language schools, like Berlitz and Linguarama, run in-house training. You are then tied to working in that organisation, but it dispenses with the need for a certificate. There are more opportunities for untrained teachers in some geographical areas, too – there is huge demand in Eastern Europe, and apparently getting a job in the Far East and Asia is easier if you are actually there. The JET programme which places graduates (preferably with PGCEs or some teaching experience) in teaching posts in Japan is well established, and can be contacted at the JET programme desk, Council on International Educational Exchange, 33 Seymour Place, London W1H 6AT; tel. 0171 224 8896.

For all sorts of TEFL posts, look in the monthly *EFL Gazette* (subscriptions from EFL Ltd, 10 Wrights Lane, Kensington, London W8 6TA; tel. 0171 937 6506), the *TES* foreign jobs section, and the *Guardian* on Tuesdays and Saturdays. The big language organisations usually have vacancy lists for their own schools, so contact them to see what's going too.

In theory, it should also be possible to teach English in a state school in the EU, as EU countries should recognise each other's professional qualifications. To see whether this is possible in practice, ring the embassy of the country in which you are interested. Do the same if you want to work in a state school of a non-EC country, but remember that organised teacher exchanges will dispense with the likely wrangles over work permits or qualifications.

Appendix A
Useful Addresses

CHAPTER 1

The Association for Science Education, College Lane, Hatfield, Hertfordshire L10 9AA; tel. 01707 267411

National Society for Education in Art and Design, The Gatehouse, Corsham Court, Corsham, Wiltshire SN13 0BZ; tel. 01249 714825

The Design and Technology Association, 16 Wellesbourne House, Walton Road, Wellesbourne, Warwickshire CV35 9JB; tel. 01789 470007

The Schools Music Association, c/o Maxwell Pryce, 71 Margaret Road, Barnet EN4 9NT; tel. 0181 440 6919

Association for Language Learning, 150 Railway Terrace, Rugby, Warwickshire, CV21 3HN; tel. 01788 546443

National Association for Special Educational Needs, 4/5 Amber Business Village, Amber Close, Amington, Tamworth, Staffordshire B77 4RP; tel. 01827 311500

The Historical Association, 59a Kennington Park Road, London SE11 4JH; tel. 0171 735 3901

The Mathematical Association, 259 London Road, Leicestershire LE2 3BE; tel. 0116 2703877

The Association of Teachers of Mathematics, 7 Shaftesbury Street, Derby DE23 8YB; tel. 01332 346599

The National Association for the Teaching of English, 50 Broadfield Road, Sheffield S8 0XJ; tel. 0114 2555296

The Geographic Association, 343 Fulwood Road, Sheffield S10 3BP; tel. 0114 2670666

The Physical Education Association, Suite 5, Churchill Square, Kings Hill, West Malling, Kent ME19 4DU; tel. 01732 875888

The National Association for the Teaching of Drama, c/o Sorrel Oates, 13 Austin Street, Northampton NN1 3EY; tel. 01604 471042

Professional Council for Religious Education, Royal Buildings, Victoria Street, Derby DE1 1GW; tel. 01332 296655

Association for the Teaching of the Social Sciences, PO Box 461, Sheffield S2 2RH; tel. 01923 213788

Joint Association of Classical Teachers, 31/34 Gordon Square, London WC1H 0PY

National Association of Teachers of Home Economics and Technology, Hamilton House, Mabledon Place, London WC1H 9BJ; tel. 0171 387 1441

Earth Science Teachers' Association, c/o The Geological Society, Burlington House, Piccadilly, London W1V 0JU; tel. 0171 434 9944

The Economics and Business Education Association, 1a Keymer Road, Hassocks, West Sussex BN6 8AD; tel. 01273 846033; e-mail ebeah@pavilion.co.uk

National Association for Pastoral Care in Education, c/o Institute of Education, The University of Warwick, Coventry CV4 7AL; tel. 01203 523810

CHAPTER 2

The Teacher Training Agency Communication Centre, PO Box 3210, Chelmsford, Essex CM1 3WA; tel. 01245 454454
E-mail: teaching@ttainfo.demon.co.uk
Internet: http://ww.teach.org.uk

Useful Addresses

The TTA will send the following publications on request:

Brochures
Routes into Teaching 96/97
Primary Teaching 96/97
Secondary Teaching 96/97
Switch to Teaching *(4-page leaflet)*

Handouts
GCSE and Equivalent Entry Qualifications
A level and Equivalent Entry to ITT
HND and Equivalent Entry to ITT
Degree Entry onto Postgraduate ITT
School Centred Initial Teacher Training (SCITT)
Nursery Nursing
Access To Higher Education
Teaching Children with Special Educational Needs
Teaching English as a Foreign Language (TEFL)
First Appointment *(for recently qualified teachers)*
Applying and Preparing for Interview for Entry to ITT
The Licensed Teacher Scheme
The Overseas Trained Teacher Scheme
Priority Subject Recruitment Scheme
Communication Centre Business Cards

Department for Education and Employment (DfEE) Publications Centre, PO Box 6927, London E3 6NZ; tel. 0171 510 0150

DfEE Teachers Qualifications Team, Mowden Hall, Staindrop Road, Darlington, County Durham DL3 9BG; tel. 01325 392120/1/2/3

DfEE Overseas Labour Service, W5 Moorfoot, Sheffield S1 4PQ; tel. 0114 259 4074

Teacher Education Admissions Clearing House, PO Box 165, Edinburgh, EH8 8AT; tel. 0131 5586169/70

General Teaching Council for Scotland, 5 Royal Terrace, Edinburgh EH7 5AF; tel. 0131 5560072

Students Awards Agency for Scotland, Gylview House, 3 Redheughs Rigg, South Gyle, Edinburgh EH12 9YT (undergraduates); postcode EH12 9YS (postgraduates); tel. 0131 244 5813 (undergraduates); 0131 244 5847 (postgraduates)

Department for Education in Northern Ireland, Teachers Branch, Waterside House, 75 Duke Street, Londonderry BT47 1FP; tel. 01514 319000

University and College Admissions Service (UCAS), Fulton House, Jessop Avenue, Cheltenham, Gloucestershire GL50 3SH; tel. 01242 222444

Graduate Teacher Training Registry (GTTR), address as UCAS; tel. 01242 225868

Open University, Walton Hall, Milton Keynes MK7 6AA

NAFTHE, 27 Britannia Street, London WC1X 9JP; tel. 0171 837 3636

SCITT courses, contact the TTA, address as above.

Licensed, Registered and Overseas Trained Teacher Schemes (England), 1 Princes Road, Ferndown, Dorset BH22 9JG; tel. 01202 897691

Licensed, Registered and Overseas Trained Teacher Schemes (Wales), The Welsh Office, FHEI Division, Cathays Park, Cardiff CF1 3NQ; tel. 01222 825831

Disability contacts

RADAR (The Royal Association for Disability and Rehabilitation), 12 City Forum, 250 City Road, London EC1V 8AF; tel. 0171 250 3222. For guides on employment rights in general, some particularly aimed at teachers, and information on equipment discounts. The Association of Disabled Professionals is at 170 Benton Hill, Horbury, Wakefield, West Yorks. WF4 5HW; tel. 01924 270335

SKILL (The National Bureau for Students with Disability), 336 Brixton Road, London SW9 77A; tel. 0171 274 0565

Useful Addresses

Access Committees all advise on access to premises. Contact Access Committee for England at 35 Great Smith Street, London SW1P 3BJ, tel. 0171 233 2566; Access Committee for Wales at Llys Ifor, Crescent Road, Caerffili, Mid Glamorgan CF8 1XL, tel. 01222 887325; or East Belfast Access Group, c/o A. Lennox, 28 Rosebery Street, Bloomfield, Belfast BT5 5BU, tel. 01232 656897

Association of Blind and Partially Sighted Teachers and Students is at BM Box 6727, London WC1N 3XX, tel. 01484 517954; and the RNIB (Royal National Institute for the Blind) at 22 Great Portland Street, London W1N 6AA, tel. 0171 388 1266

Contact the Hearing Impaired Group through the Royal National Institute for the Deaf, 105 Gower Street, London WC1E 6AH, tel. 0171 436 9769; or write to the co-ordinator at Studio 4, 47 Wharfdale Road, London N1 9SE

CHAPTER 3

To contact local education authorities and local schools, go directly to your local library and get your hands on *The Education Year Book*, published and updated annually by Pitman. This will have the precise local addresses you need for targeting most of the information sources mentioned in chapter 3, and will probably also name the individual who deals with your area of interest.

The Northern Irish management committees are:

Controlled schools
Chief Executive, Belfast Education & Library Board, 40 Academy Street, Belfast BT1 2NQ; tel. 01232 564000

Chief Executive, Western Education & Library Board, Campsie House, 1 Hospital Road, Omagh, Co. Tyrone BT79 0AW; tel. 01662 240240

Chief Executive, North-Eastern Education & Library Board, County Hall, 182 Galgorm Road, Ballymena, Co. Antrim BT42 1HN; tel. 01266 653333

Chief Executive, South-Eastern Education & Library Board, 18 Windsor Avenue, Belfast BT9 6EF; tel. 01232 381188

Chief Executive, Southern Education & Library Board, 3 Charlemont Place, Armagh BT61 9AX; tel. 01861 512200

Maintained schools
Council for Catholic Maintained Schools, 160 High Street, Holywood, Co. Down BT18 9HT; tel. 01232 426972

The Scottish EAs are:

Aberdeen City Council, Town House, Aberdeen AB9 1AQ; tel. 01224 522502

Aberdeenshire Council, c/o Woodhill House, Westburn Road, Aberdeen AB9 2LU; tel. 01224 665106

Angus Council, 7 The Cross, Forfar DD8 1BX; tel. 01307 461460

Argyll and Bute Council, Argyll House, Alexandra Parade, Dunoon PA23 8AJ; tel. 01369 704000

Clackmannanshire Council, Greenfield, Alloa FK10 2AD; tel. 01259 450000

Dumfries and Galloway Council, Department of Education, 30 Edinburgh Road, Dumfries DG1 1JQ; tel. 01387 260418

Dundee City Council, 21 City Square, Dundee DD1 3BY; tel. 01382 434000

East Ayrshire Council, London Road Centre, London Road, Kilmarnock KA3 7DG; tel. 01563 574057

East Dunbartonshire Council, Tom Johnston House, Civic Way, Kirkintilloch G66 4TJ; tel. 0141 776 7171

East Lothian Council, Haddington House, Haddington EH41 4BU; tel. 01620 826789

East Renfrewshire Council, c/o Strathclyde Regional Council, Strathclyde House 2, 20 India Street, Glasgow G2 4PF; tel. 0141 227 3852

Useful Addresses

City of Edinburgh Council, c/o 40 Torphichen Street, Edinburgh EH3 8JJ; tel. 0131 229 9166

Falkirk Council, Municipal Buildings, Falkirk FK1 5RS; tel. 01324 624911

Fife Council, Fife House, North Street, Glenrothes KY7 5LT; tel. 01592 414141

City of Glasgow Council, Education Department, Education Offices, 129 Bath Street, Glasgow G2 2SY; tel. 0141 204 2900

Highland Council, Regional Building, Glenurquhart Road, Inverness IV3 5NX; tel. 01463 702831

Inverclyde Council, Municipal Buildings, Greenock PA15 1LY; tel. 01475 882701

Midlothian Council, Midlothian House, Buccleuch Street, Dalkeith EH22 1DJ; tel. 0131 663 2881

Moray Council, Council Headquarters, High Street, Elgin IV30 1BX; tel. 01343 543451

North Ayrshire Council, Cunninghame House, Irvine KA12 8EE; tel. 01294 271334

North Lanarkshire Council, Regional Offices, Almada Street, Hamilton ML3 0AE; tel. 01698 266166

Orkney Islands Council, Council Offices, Kirkwall, Orkney KW15 1NY; tel. 01856 873535

Perthshire and Kinross Council, Education Department, 6–8 South Methven Street, Perth PH1 5PF; tel. 01738 38101

Renfrewshire Council, 16 Glasgow Road, Paisley PA1 3QG; tel. 0141 887 8212

Scottish Borders Council, Regional Headquarters, Newtown St Boswells, Melrose TD6 0SA; tel. 01835 823301

Shetland Islands Council, Town Hall, Lerwick; tel. 01595 693535

South Ayrshire Council, PO Box 1996, Wellington Square, Ayr KA7 1DS; tel. 01292 612000

South Lanarkshire Council, Council Building, Almada Street, Hamilton ML3 0AA; tel. 01698 454517

Stirling Council, Viewforth, Stirling FK8 2ET; tel. 01786 442000

West Dunbartonshire Council, Garshake Road, Dumbarton G82 3PU; tel. 01389 727580

West Lothian Council, District Headquarters, South Bridge Street, Bathgate EH48 1TS; tel. 01506 637000

Western Isles Council, Council Offices, Sandwich Road, Stornoway, Isle of Lewis HS1 2BW; tel. 01851 703773

The General Teaching Council for Scotland, 5 Royal Terrace, Edinburgh EH7 5AF; tel. 0131 556 0072

The Scottish Office Education and Industry Department, Victoria Quay, Edinburgh EH6 6QQ; tel. 0131 556 8400

Local and regional wings of your union can be tracked down from membership details, or from union head offices at:

National Union of Teachers, Hamilton House, Mabledon Place, London WC1H 9BD; tel. 0171 388 6191

National Association of Schoolteachers/Union of Women Teachers, Hillscourt Education Centre, Rose Hill, Rednal, Birmingham B45 RS; tel. 0121 453 6150

Association of Teachers and Lecturers, 7 Northumberland Street, London WC2N 5DA; tel. 0171 930 6441

Professional Association of Teachers, 18 Gadwall Croft, Birmingham B23; tel. 0132 372337

Undeb Cenedlaethol Athrawon Cymru, Pen Roc, Rhodfa'r Môr, Aberystwyth, Ceredigion SY23 2AZ; tel. 01970 615577

Educational Institute of Scotland, 46 Moray Place, Edinburgh EH3 6BH; tel. 0131 225 6244

Addresses relevant to the section on Independent Schools are:

Girls' Schools Association, 130 Regent Road, Leicester LE1 7PA; tel. 0116 254 1619

Headmasters' and Headmistresses' Conference, address as GSA above; tel. 0116 285 4810

Independent Schools Association, Boys' British School, East Street, Saffron Walden, Essex CB10 1LS; tel. 01799 523619

Gabbitas Educational Consultants, Carrington House, 126–130 Regent Street, London W1R 6EE; tel. 0171 734 0161

QED, 90 Gloucester Place, London W1H 4BL; tel. 0171 935 4909

START, 132 Heathfield Road, Keston, Kent BR2 6BA; tel. 01689 855575

School Appointment Service, 22 Peter's Close, Prestwood, Bucks HP16 9ET; tel. 01494 863027

DfEE Publications Centre, Great Smith Street, London SW1P 3BT; tel. 0171 925 5000

CHAPTER 6

The Central Bureau for Educational Visits and Exchanges
England: Seymour Mews House, Seymour Mews, London W1H 9PE; tel. 0171 486 5101
Scotland: 3 Bruntsfield Crescent, Edinburgh EH10 4HD; tel. 0131 447 8024
Northern Ireland: 16 Malone Road, Belfast BT9 5BN; tel. 0232 664418

League for the Exchange of Commonwealth Teachers, Commonwealth House, 7 Lion Yard, Tremadoc Road, Clapham, London SW4 7NQ; tel. 0171 498 1101

British Council, Overseas Educational Appointments Department, Medlock Street, Manchester M15 4AA; *and*

British Council, Central Management of Direct Teaching, 10 Spring Gardens, London SW1A 2BN; tel. 0171 389 4931

RSA, Westwood Way, Coventry CV4 8HS; tel. 01203 470033

Trinity College London, 16 Park Crescent, London W1N 4AH; tel. 0171 323 2328

EFL Ltd, 10 Wrights Lane, Kensington, London W8 6TA; tel. 0171 937 6506

Appendix B
Points Systems and Pay Scales

PAY RANGES FOR HEADTEACHERS AND DEPUTY HEADTEACHERS UNTIL 30 NOVEMBER 1998 AND FROM 1 DECEMBER 1999

Headteachers

School group	Spine point	Pay range until 30 November 1998 (£)	Pay range from 1 December 1998 (£)
1	3–15	26,733–31,821	27,204–32,382
2 1(S)	8–22	28,848–35,070	29,355–35,691
3 2(S)	15–29	31,821–39,036	32,382–39,726
4 3(S)	23–37	35,640–44,694	36,270–45,483
5 4(S)	31–44	40,449–51,621	41,163–52,533
6	38–51	45,684–58,548	46,488–59,580

Deputy headteachers

School group	Spine point	Pay range until 30 November 1998 (£)	Pay range from 1 December 1998 (£)
1	1–8	25,881–28,848	26,337–29,355
2 1(S)	2–10	26,307–29,703	26,772–30,228
3 2(S)	4–13	27,159–30,966	27,636–31,515
4 3(S)	8–20	28,848–33,942	29,355–34,539
5 4(S)	15–26	31,821–37,335	32,382–37,995
6	22–34	35,070–42,573	35,691–43,326

PAY SPINE FOR ADVANCED SKILLS TEACHERS FROM 1 SEPTEMBER 1998

Spine point	Annual salary from 1 September 1998 (£)
1	25,200
2	25,650
3	26,100
4	26,550
5	27,000
6	27,450
7	27,900
8	28,350
9	28,800
10	29,250
11	29,700
12	30,300
13	30,900
14	31,500
15	32,100
16	32,700
17	33,300
18	33,900
19	34,500
20	35,100
21	35,700
22	36,450
23	37,200
24	37,950
25	38,700
26	39,450
27	40,200

PAY SPINE FOR CLASSROOM TEACHERS UNTIL 30 NOVEMBER 1998 AND FROM 1 DECEMBER 1998

Spine point	Annual salary until 30 November 1998 (£)	Annual salary from 1 December 1998 (£)
0	13,131	13,362
0.5	13,518	13,758
1	13,917	14,163
1.5	14,331	14,583
2	14,751	15,012
2.5	15,150	15,417
3	15,555	15,828
3.5	15,969	16,251
4	16,398	16,689
4.5	16,878	17,178
5	17,379	17,685
5.5	17,895	18,210
6	18,423	18,750

6.5	18,969	19,305
7	19,530	19,875
7.5	20,106	20,463
8	20,700	21,066
8.5	21,351	21,726
9	22,023	22,410
9.5	22,695	23,097
10	23,385	23,796
10.5	24,069	24,495
11	24,777	25,215
11.5	25,746	26,202
12	26,754	27,225
12.5	27,633	28,119
13	28,539	29,040
13.5	29,658	30,180
14	30,816	31,362
14.5	31,503	32,058
15	32,199	32,769
15.5	32,919	33,501
16	33,654	34,248
16.5	34,401	35,007
17	35,166	35,787

Point 2 is the minimum starting salary of a newly qualified teacher with a good honours degree

BASIS ON WHICH PAY SPINE POINTS ARE AWARDED TO CLASSROOM TEACHERS

Position on the pay spine is determined by the total of the points (up to a maximum of 17 full points) awarded by governing bodies in respect of:

- ***Qualifications*** – 2 full points for a second class honours degree or better;

- ***Experience*** – 1 full point for each year of service up to a maximum of 9 (7 for those with the 2 points for qualifications), subject to governing bodies' discretion to discount unsatisfactory service. Governing bodies may award extra full or half points for years of relevant experience outside teaching (within the overall maximum of 7 or 9 full points);

- ***Responsibilities*** – full or half points up to a maximum of 5 full points for undertaking defined extra responsibilities. To be awarded while holding a particular post or on a short-term basis at the discretion of governing bodies;

- **Excellence** – full or half points up to a maximum of 3 full points for performance in all duties but with particular regard to quality of classroom teaching. To be awarded on an annual basis at the discretion of governing bodies;

- **Recruitment and retention** – full or half points up to a maximum of 2 full points (3 full points in the inner London allowance area) to ease particular recruitment and retention problems. To be awarded at the discretion of governing bodies, subject to biennial review; and

- **Special needs** – up to 2 full points while teaching pupils with special educational needs (in special or mainstream schools), on the following basis:

    • the *first special needs point* is mandatory for classroom teachers in special schools and for classroom teachers in ordinary schools who are engaged wholly or mainly in teaching pupils with statements of special educational needs. Governing bodies can also award the first point on a discretionary basis to classroom teachers in ordinary schools who are engaged wholly or mainly in teaching pupils with special educational needs, none or not all of whom have statements; and

    • a *second special needs full or half point* may be awarded by governing bodies to teachers whose special needs experience or qualifications are particularly relevant to their work.

Points awarded for qualifications and experience become a permanent entitlement for the individual concerned. Other points are not permanent additions to pay, but are held on the basis indicated under each criterion.

Acknowledgements

Thanks to all the named individuals in the text for their time, and for entertaining Elis whilst they talked. Thanks to Gemma Sheridan and staff at Hendon School, Faith Woodruff and staff at Elliot School, Lil Llewelyn and staff at Winston Churchill School, and Keith Mitchell and staff at John Smeaton School, for sharing their career experiences and advice. Thanks to anyone else who also recognises their CV or comments.

I am grateful to the following people for advice, information and practical help: Eilian and Sian James, Salli Vandyck, Ann Mannion, Emma Randall, Jane McNeill, Lyn Stephenson, Mark Homer, Tanya Whatling and numerous officers at the DfEE, TTA and NUT, NASUWT and NAHT. Thanks very much to Clive Priddle.

Most of all, thanks to the boys at home, for putting up with all this with their usual good humour.

Also available in the Guardian Careers Guide Series from Fourth Estate:

FURTHER AND ADULT EDUCATION

Peter Mayhew-Smith

A vital sector, newly emphasised by government as essential for stimulating and sharpening a professional workforce, this guide is to careers in teaching in adult and further education.

Outside full-time education there seems to be nothing but a confusion of acronyms. This book explains, quantifies and appraises the entire further education sector including: FE colleges, Colleges of Tertiary Education; 6th Form Colleges; Adult Education Colleges; Community Education Services; TECs; Supply Agencies; Private Training Agencies; and the newly designated University of Industry. With advice and guidance on pay, career structure, the various employers in the sector, training, getting started, choosing what to teach and at what level, pastoral work, counselling and the full range of the teacher's duties, and shifting within and out from the sector this book presents a complete and comprehensive overview of careers in adult and further education.

£8.99   ISBN: 1 85702 545 8

ACCOUNTANCY

Sarah Perrin

The guide to the wide-ranging careers possible with an accountancy qualification.

Traditionally seen as one of the least exciting but safest career areas, accountancy skills are now required in all manner of businesses from the City to charities, schools and hospitals. This book explains the enviable range of options from working for a professional partnership to climbing the corporate ladder; from working in the public sector to self-employment.

£8.99   ISBN: 1 85702 751 5

JOBFINDER

Christine Ingham

The essential guide to finding employment for those entering the job market and those planning a career change.

The world of work has changed: most people will work for several employers in the course of their careers. To the new, would-be employee, or someone wanting to shift career, this is an uncertain universe in which to pitch one's qualifications. It demands new skills, a willingness to be adaptable and an initial resourcefulness in learning where opportunities are to be found and how best to exploit them. This guide will provide essential answers to all the most difficult questions that may arise in this new climate.

£8.99   ISBN: 1 85702 630 6

INTERVIEWS

Christine Ingham

How to prepare yourself fully for the most important part of the job application process: the face-to-face interview.

The interview is of prime importance. It's the moment when you must impress personality, fluency, interest and some guile if necessary. This book tells you how to prepare for every eventuality. It breaks down the kind of questions you are likely to meet and gives examples of the most typical. It discusses the different strategies you might adopt when faced with a panel of interviewers rather than a single one. Also, crucially, it explains how you should use the interview for your own ends: how to take control of the direction it is following, and how to put the interviewer on the spot.

£8.99   ISBN: 1 85702 627 6

NEWS JOURNALISM

Nick Varley

The guide to working with the news: from local paper reporter to satellite television newscaster.

Media studies courses have blossomed and competition for places on them – never mind jobs afterwards – is intense. This book is targeted at those people for whom the news is their specific ambition. The interchangeability of skills and the flexibility now required of news journalists so that they can flit between radio and television are essential qualities to have. The book examines the core abilities required of a good news reporter and news editor, and the pitfalls of a profession that is built around the contact book.

£8.99   ISBN: 1 85702 693 4

LAW

Fiona Boyle

The guide to all legal careers from the most modest legal-aid barrister to the most affluent corporate solicitor.

The law continues to attract waves of applicants in search of a career in one of the classic professions. This guide outlines all the various specialisations available within the law. It looks at which areas of work are expanding and which contracting, follows the careers of successful young lawyers, looks at paralegal openings and examines the flexibility of a legal qualification and its suitability for other areas of work. Focusing primarily on careers in the law in England and Wales, it also includes details of the different legal set-ups in Scotland and Northern Ireland and advice on European and overseas career opportunities.

£8.99   ISBN: 1 85702 631 4

All Fourth Estate books are available at your local bookshop or newsagent, or can be ordered direct from the publisher.

Indicate the number of copies required and quote the author and title.

Send cheque/eurocheque/postal order (Sterling only), made payable to Book Service By Post, to:

> Fourth Estate Books,
> Book Service By Post,
> PO Box 29, Douglas
> I-O-M, IM99 1BQ

Or phone: 01624 675137

Or fax: 01624 670923

Or e-mail: bookshop@enterprise.net

Alternatively pay by Access, Visa or Mastercard

Card number

Expiry date ....

Signature ....

Post and packing is free in the UK. Overseas customers please allow £1.00 per book for post and packing.

Name
Address

Please allow 28 days for delivery. Please tick the box if you do not wish to receive any additional information. ❑

Prices and availability subject to change without notice.